Workshop on Interactive Language Learning, Visualization and Interfaces 2014

AA005865

Held at ACL 2014

Baltimore, Maryland, USA
27 June 2014

ISBN: 978-1-63439-211-2

Printed from e-media with permission by:

Curran Associates, Inc.
57 Morehouse Lane
Red Hook, NY 12571

Some format issues inherent in the e-media version may also appear in this print version.

Copyright© (2014) by the Association for Computational Linguistics
All rights reserved.

Printed by Curran Associates, Inc. (2014)

For permission requests, please contact the Association for Computational Linguistics at the address below.

Association for Computational Linguistics
209 N. Eighth Street
Stroudsburg, Pennsylvania 18360

Phone: 1-570-476-8006
Fax: 1-570-476-0860

acl@aclweb.org

Additional copies of this publication are available from:

Curran Associates, Inc.
57 Morehouse Lane
Red Hook, NY 12571 USA
Phone: 845-758-0400
Fax: 845-758-2634
Email: curran@proceedings.com
Web: www.proceedings.com

Title Sponsor: Idibon

idibon

language technologies for
a connected world

Introduction

People acquire language through social interaction. Computers learn linguistic models from data, and increasingly, from language-based exchange with people. How do computational linguistic techniques and interactive visualizations work in concert to improve linguistic data processing for humans and computers? How can statistical learning models be best paired with interactive interfaces? How can the increasing quantity of linguistic data be better explored and analyzed? These questions span statistical natural language processing (NLP), human-computer interaction (HCI), and information visualization (Vis), three fields with natural connections but infrequent meetings. Vis and HCI are niches in NLP; Vis and HCI have not fully utilized the statistical techniques developed in NLP. This workshop aims to assemble an interdisciplinary community that promotes collaboration across these fields.

Three themes define this first workshop:

Active, Online, and Interactive Machine Learning Statistical machine learning (ML) has yielded tremendous gains in coverage and robustness for many tasks, but there is a growing sense that additional error reduction might require a fresh look at the human role. Presently, human inputs are often restricted to passive annotation in ML research. However, the fields of ML and HCI are both developing new techniques—such as active learning, incremental/online learning, and crowdsourcing—that attempt to engage people in novel and productive ways. How do we jointly solve the learning questions that have been the domain of NLP and address research topics in HCI such as managing human workers and increasing the quality of their responses?

Language-based user interfaces NLP techniques have entered mainstream use, but the field currently focuses more on building and improving systems and less on understanding how users interact with them in real-world environments. User interface (UI) design decisions can affect the perceived or actual performance of a system. For example, while machine translation (MT) quality improved considerably over the last decade, studies found that human translators disliked MT output for reasons unrelated to translation quality. Many existing systems present sentence-level translations in the absence of relevant context, and disrupt rather than contribute to a translator's workflow. How do we best integrate learning methods, user behavior understanding, and human-centered design methodology?

Text Visualization and Analysis The quantity and diversity of linguistic corpora is swelling. Recent work on visualizing text data annotated with linguistic structures (e.g., syntactic trees, hypergraphs, and sequences) has produced tools that enable exploration of thematic and recurrence patterns in text. Visual representations built on the outputs of word-level models (e.g., sentiment classifiers, topic models, and continuous word embedding models) now power exploratory analysis of legal documents, political text, and social media content. Beyond adding analytic value, interactive visualization can also reduce the upfront effort needed to set up, configure, and learn a tool, as well as promote adoption. How do we pair appropriate NLP techniques and visualizations to assist both expert and non-technical users, who encounter a growing amount of linguistic data in their professional and everyday lives?

Organizers

Jason Chuang	University of Washington (USA)
Spence Green	Stanford University (USA)
Marti Hearst	UC Berkeley (USA)
Jeffrey Heer	University of Washington (USA)
Philipp Koehn	Johns Hopkins University (USA)

Program Committee

Vicente Alabau	Robin Hill
Cecilia Aragon	Eser Kandogan
Chris Callison-Burch	Frank Keller
Francisco Casacuberta	Katie Kuksenok
Allison Chaney	Laurens van der Maaten
Christopher Collins	Christopher D. Manning
John DeNero	Aditi Muralidharan
Marian Dörk	Burr Settles
Jacob Eisenstein	John Stasko
Jim Herbsleb	Fernanda Viégas

Martin Wattenberg

Invited Speakers

Chris Culy	Universität Tübingen
Marti Hearst	UC Berkeley
Jimmy Lin	University of Maryland, College Park
Noah Smith	Carnegie Mellon University
Krist Wongsuphasawat	Twitter

Table of Contents

Conference Program

Friday June 27, 2014

8:30 **Opening Remarks**

8:45 **Invited Talk**
Jimmy Lin

Research Papers

9:30 *MiTextExplorer: Linked brushing and mutual information for exploratory text data analysis*
Brendan O'Connor

9:50 *Interactive Learning of Spatial Knowledge for Text to 3D Scene Generation*
Angel Chang, Manolis Savva and Christopher Manning

10:10 *Dynamic Wordclouds and Vennclouds for Exploratory Data Analysis*
Glen Coppersmith and Erin Kelly

10:30 **Coffee Break**

11:00 **Invited Talk**
Noah Smith

11:45 **Invited Talk**
Marti Hearst

12:30 **Lunch Break**

2:00 **Invited Talk**
Chris Culy

2:45 **Interactive Demo Session**

Active Learning with Constrained Topic Model
Yi Yang, Shimei Pan, Doug Downey and Kunpeng Zhang

GLANCE Visualizes Lexical Phenomena for Language Learning
MeiHua Chen, Shih-Ting Huang, Ting-Hui Kao, Hsun-wen Chiu and Tzu-Hsi Yen

SPIED: Stanford Pattern based Information Extraction and Diagnostics
Sonal Gupta and Christopher Manning

Interactive Exploration of Asynchronous Conversations: Applying a User-centered Approach to Design a Visual Text Analytic System
Enamul Hoque, Giuseppe Carenini and Shafiq Joty

Friday June 27, 2014 (continued)

Interactive Demo Session (continued)

MUCK: A toolkit for extracting and visualizing semantic dimensions of large text collections
Rebecca Weiss

Design of an Active Learning System with Human Correction for Content Analysis
Nancy McCracken, Jasy Suet Yan Liew and Kevin Crowston

LDAvis: A method for visualizing and interpreting topics
Carson Sievert and Kenneth Shirley

Hiearchie: Visualization for Hierarchical Topic Models
Alison Smith, Timothy Hawes and Meredith Myers

Concurrent Visualization of Relationships between Words and Topics in Topic Models
Alison Smith, Jason Chuang, Yuening Hu, Jordan Boyd-Graber and Leah Findlater

4:00 **Invited Talk**
Krist Wongsuphasawat

4:45 **Discussion and Closing Remarks**

MITEXTEXPLORER: Linked brushing and mutual information for exploratory text data analysis

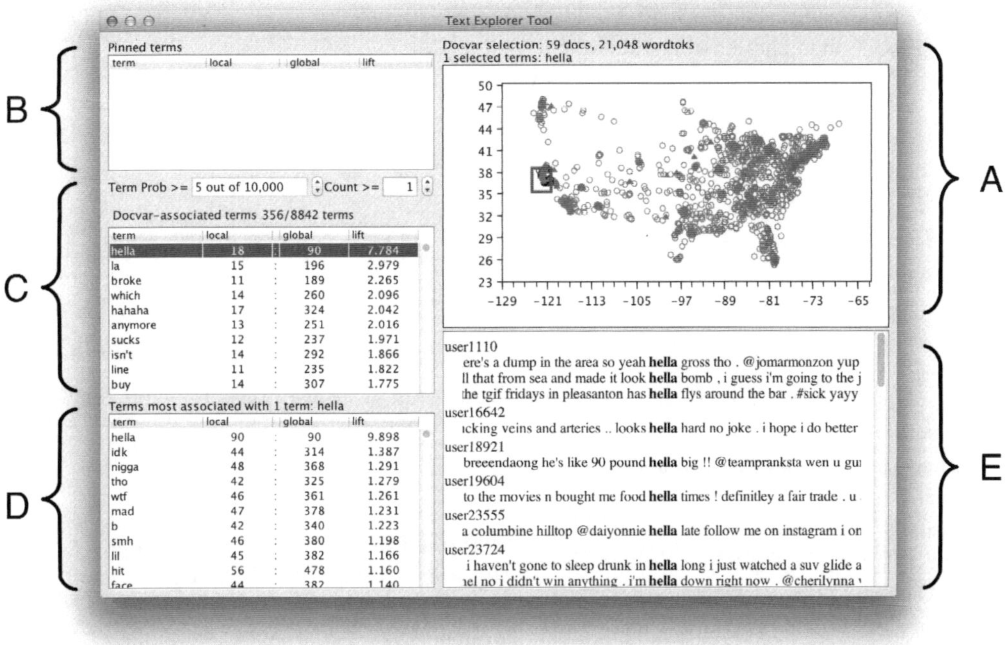

Figure 1: Screenshot of MITEXTEXPLORER, analyzing geolocated tweets.

Brendan O'Connor
Machine Learning Department
Carnegie Mellon University
brenocon@cs.cmu.edu
http://brenocon.com

Abstract

In this paper I describe a preliminary experimental system, MITEXTEXPLORER, for *textual linked brushing*, which allows an analyst to interactively explore statistical relationships between (1) terms, and (2) document metadata (covariates). An analyst can graphically select documents embedded in a temporal, spatial, or other continuous space, and the tool reports terms with strong statistical associations for the region. The user can then drill down to specific term and term groupings, viewing further associations, and see how terms are used in context. The goal is to rapidly compare language usage across interesting document covariates.

I illustrate examples of using the tool on several datasets: geo-located Twitter messages, presidential State of the Union addresses, the ACL Anthology, and the King James Bible.

1 Introduction: Can we "just look" at statistical text data?

Exploratory data analysis (EDA) is an approach to extract meaning from data, which emphasizes learning about a dataset through an iterative process of many analyses which suggest and refine possible hypotheses. It is vital in early stages of a data analysis for data cleaning and sanity checks, which are crucial to help ensure a dataset will be useful. Exploratory techniques can also suggest possible hypotheses or issues for further investigation.

Proceedings of the Workshop on Interactive Language Learning, Visualization, and Interfaces, pages 1–13,
Baltimore, Maryland, USA, June 27, 2014. ©2014 Association for Computational Linguistics

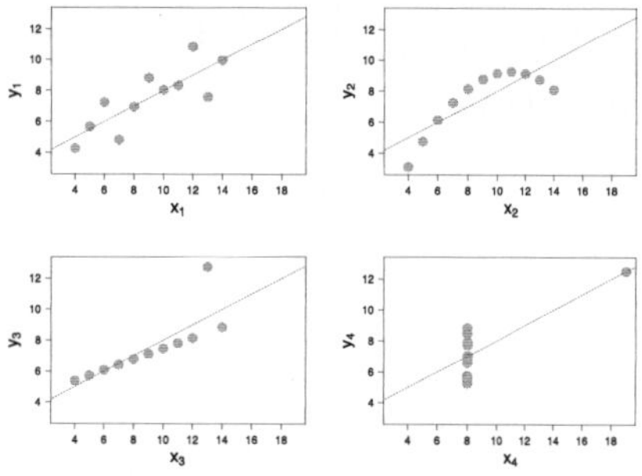

Figure 2: Anscombe Quartet. (Source: Wikipedia)

The classical approach to EDA, as pioneered in works such as Tukey (1977) and Cleveland (1993) (and other work from the Bell Labs statistics group during that period) emphasizes visual analysis under nonparametric, model-free assumptions, in which visual attributes are a fairly direct reflection of numerical or categorical aspects of data. As a simple example, consider the well-known Anscombe Quartet (1973), a set of four bivariate example datasets. The Pearson correlation, a very widely used measure of dependence that assumes a linear Gaussian model of the data, finds that each dataset has an identical amount of dependence ($r = 0.82$). However, a scatterplot instantly reveals that very different dependence relationships hold in each dataset (Figure 2). The scatterplot is possibly the simplest visual analysis tool for investigating the relationship between two variables, in which the variables' numerical values are mapped to horizontal and vertical space. While the correlation coefficient is a model-based analysis tool, the scatterplot is model-free (or at least, it is effective under an arguably wider range of data generating assumptions), which is crucial for this example.

This nonparametric, visual approach to EDA has been encoded into many data analysis packages, including the now-ubiquitous R language (R Core Team, 2013), which descends from earlier software by the Bell Labs statistics group (Becker and Chambers, 1984). In R, tools such as histograms, boxplots, barplots, dotplots, mosaicplots, etc. are built-in, basic operators in the language. (Wilkinson (2006)'s grammar of graphics more extensively systematizes this approach; see also (Wickham, 2010; Bostock et al., 2011).)

In the meantime, *textual data* has emerged as a resource of increasing interest for many scientific, business, and government data analysis applications. Consider the use case of automated content analysis (a.k.a. text mining) as a tool for investigating social scientific and humanistic questions (Grimmer and Stewart, 2013; Jockers, 2013; Shaw, 2012; O'Connor et al., 2011). The content of the data is under question: analysts are interested in what/when/how/by-whom different concepts, ideas, or attitudes are expressed in a corpus, and the trends in these factors across time, space, author communities, or other document-level covariates (often called metadata). Comparisons of word statistics across covariates are absolutely essential to many interesting questions or social measurement problems, such as

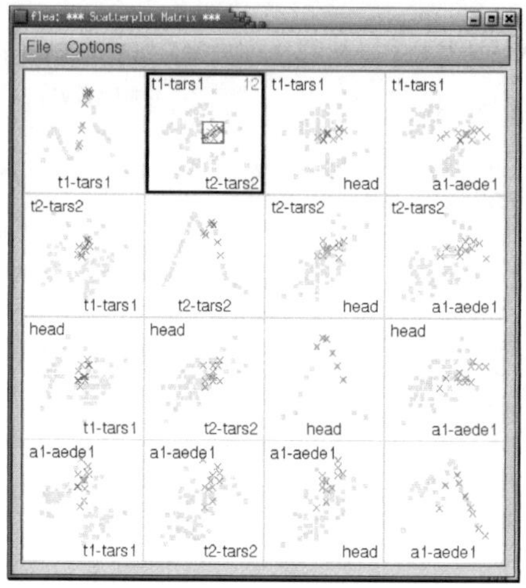

Figure 3: Linked brushing with the analysis software *GGobi*. More references at source: `http://www.infovis-wiki.net/index.php?title=Linking_and_Brushing`

- What topics tend to get censored by the Chinese government online, and why (Bamman et al., 2012; King et al., 2013)? *Covariates*: whether a message is deleted by censors, time/location of message.

- What drives media bias? Do newspapers slant their coverage in response to what readers want (Gentzkow and Shapiro, 2010)? *Covariates*: political preferences of readers, competitiveness of media markets.

There exist dozens, if not more, of other examples in social scientific and humanities research; see references in O'Connor et al. (2011); O'Connor (2014).

In this work, I focus on the question: What

should be the baseline exploratory tools for textual data, to discover important statistical associations between *text* and *document covariates*? Ideally, we'd like to "just look" at the data, in the spirit of scatterplotting the Anscombe Quartet. An analysis tool to support this should not require any statistical model assumptions, and should display the data in as direct a form as possible.

For low-dimensional, non-textual data, the base functionality of R prescribes a broad array of useful defaults: one-dimensional continuous data can be histogrammed (*hist(x)*), or kernel density plotted (*plot(density(x))*), while the relationship between two dimensions of continuous variables can be viewed as a scatterplot (*plot(x,y)*); or perhaps a boxplot for discrete *x* and continous *y* (*boxplot(x,y)*); and so on. Commercial data analysis systems such as Excel, Stata, Tableau, JMP, etc., have similar functionality.

These visual tools can be useful for analyzing derived content statistics from text—for example, showing a high-level topic or sentiment frequency trending over time—but they cannot visualize the text itself. Text data consists of a linear sequence of high-dimensional discrete variables (words). The most aggressive and common analysis approach, bag-of-words, eliminates the problematic sequential structure, by reducing a document to a high-dimensional discrete counts over words. But still, none of the above visual tools makes sense for visualizing a word distribution; many popular tools simply crash or become very slow when given word count data. And besides the issues of discrete high-dimensionality, text is unique in that it has to be manually *read* in order to more reliably understand its meaning. Natural language processing tools can sometimes extract partial views of text meaning, but full understanding is a long ways off; and the quality of available NLP tools varies greatly across corpora and languages. A useful exploratory tool should be able to work with a variety of levels of sophistication in NLP tooling, and allow the user to fall back to manual reading when necessary.

2 MITEXTEXPLORER: linked brushing for text and covariate correlations

The analysis tool presented here, MITEXTEXPLORER, is designed for exploratory analysis of relationships between document covariates—such as time, space, or author community—against textual variables—words, or other units of meaning, that can be counted per document. Unlike topic model approaches to analyzing covariate-text relationships (Mimno, 2012; Roberts et al., 2013), there is no dimension reduction of the terms. Instead, interactivity allows a user to explore more of the high-dimensional space, by specifying a *document selection* (Q) and/or a *term selection* (T). We are inspired by the *linking and brushing* family of techniques in interactive data visualization, in which an analyst can select a group of data points under a query in one covariate space, and see the same data selection in a different covariate space (Figure 3; see Buja et al. (1996), and e.g. Becker and Cleveland (1987); Buja et al. (1991); Martin and Ward (1995); Cook and Swayne (2007)). In our case, one of the variables is text.

The interface consists of several *linked views*, which contain:

(A) a view of the documents in a two-dimensional covariate space (e.g. scatterplot),

(B) an optional list of pinned terms,

(C) *document-associated terms*: a view of the relatively most frequent terms for the current document selection,

(D) *term-associated terms*: a view of terms that relatively frequently co-occur with the current term selection; and

(E) a keyword-in-context (KWIC) display of textual passages for the current term selection.

Figure 1 shows the interface viewing a corpus of 201,647 geo-located Twitter messages from 2,000 users during 2009-2012, which have been tagged with their author's spatial coordinates through a mobile phone client and posted publicly; for data analysis, their texts have been lowercased and tokenized appropriately (Owoputi et al., 2013; O'Connor et al., 2010). Since this type of corpus contains casual, everyday language, it is a dataset that may illuminate geographic patterns of slang and lexical variation in local dialects (Eisenstein et al., 2012, 2010).

The document covariate display (A) uses (longitude, latitude) positions as the 2D space. The corpus has been preprocessed to define a document as the concatenation of messages from a single author, with its position the average location of the author's messages. When the interface loads, all points in (A) are initially gray, and all other panels are blank.

2.1 Covariate-driven queries

A core interaction, *brushing*, consists of using the mouse to select a rectangle in the (x,y) covariate space. Figure 1 shows a selection around the Bay Area metropolitan area (blue rectangle). Upon selection, the document-driven term display (C) is updated to show the relatively most frequent terms in the document selection. Let Q denote the set of documents that are selected by the current covariate query. The tool ranks terms w by their (exponentiated) pointwise mutual information, a.k.a. *lift*, for Q:

$$\text{lift}(w;Q) = \frac{p(w|Q)}{p(w)} \quad \left(= \frac{p(w,Q)}{p(w)p(Q)}\right) \tag{1}$$

This quantity measures how much more frequent the term is in the queryset, compared to the baseline global probability in the corpus ($p(w)$). Probabilities are calculated with simple MLE relative frequencies, i.e.

$$\frac{p(w|Q)}{p(w)} = \frac{\sum_{d \in Q} n_{dw}}{\sum_{d \in Q} n_d} \frac{N}{n_w} \tag{2}$$

where d denotes a document ID, n_{dw} the count of word w in document d, and N the number of tokens in the corpus. PMI gives results that are much more interesting than results from ranking w on raw probability within the query set ($p(w|Q)$), since that simply shows grammatical function words or other terms that are common both in the queryset and across the corpus, and not distinctive for the queryset.[1]

A well-known weakness of PMI is overemphasis on rare terms; terms that appear only in the queryset, even if they appear only once, will attain the highest PMI value. One way to address this is through a smoothing prior/pseudocounts/regularization, or through statistical significance ranking (see §3). For simplicity, we use a minimum frequency threshold filter. The user interface allows minimums for either local or global term frequencies, and to easily adjust them, which naturally shifts the emphasis between specific and generic language. All methods to protect against rare probabilistic events necessarily involve such a tradeoff parameter that the user ought to experiment with; given this situation, we might prefer a transparent mechanism instead of mathematical priors (though see also §3).

Figure 1 shows that *hella* is the highest ranked term for this spatial selection (and freqency threshold), occurring 7.8 times more frequently compared to the overall corpus; this comports with surveyed intuitions of Californian English speakers (Bucholtz et al., 2007). For full transparency to the user, the local and global term counts are shown in the table. (Since *hella* occurred 18 times in the queryset and 90 times globally, this implies the simple conditional probability $p(Q|w) = 18/90$; and indeed, ranking on $p(Q|w)$ is equivalent to ranking on PMI, since exponentiated PMI is $p(Q|w)/p(Q)$.) The user can also sort by local count to see the raw most-frequent term report for the document selection. As the user reshapes the query box, or drags it around the space, the terms in panel (C) are updated.

Not shown are options to change the term frequency representation. For exposition here, probabilities are formulated as counts of tokens, but this can be problematic for social media data, since a single user might use a term a very large number of times. The above analysis is conducted with an indicator representation of terms per user, so all frequencies refer to the probability that a user uses the term at least once. However, the other examples in this paper use token-level frequencies, which seem to work fine. It is an interesting statistical analysis question how to derive a single range of methods to work across these situations.

2.2 Term selection and KWIC views

Terms in the table (C) can be clicked and selected, forming a term selection as a set of terms T. This action drives several additional views:

(A) documents containing the term are highlighted in the document covariate display (here, in red),

(E) examples of the term's usage, in Keyword-in-Context style with vertical alignment for the query term; and

(D) other terms that frequently co-occur with T (§2.3).

The KWIC report in (E) shows examples of term's usage. For example, why is the term "la" in

[1] The term "lift" is used in business applications (Provost and Fawcett, 2013), while PMI has been used in many NLP applications to measure word associations.

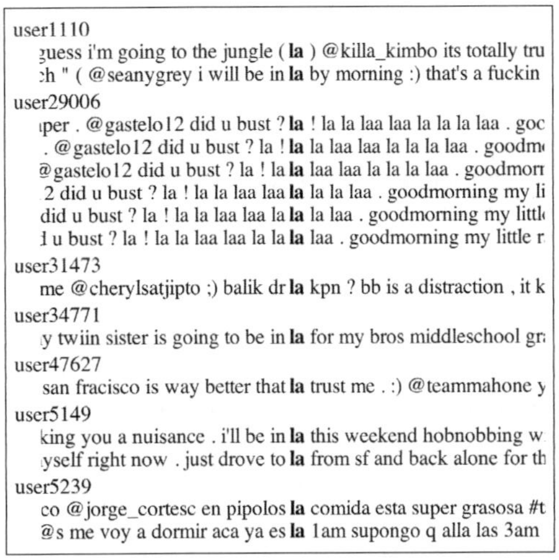

Figure 4: KWIC examples of "la" usage in tweets selected in Figure 1.

the PMI list? My initial thought was that this was an example of "LA", short for "Los Angeles". But clicking on "la" instantly disproves this hypothesis—Figure 4, showing the Los Angeles sense, but also the "la la la" sense, as well as the Spanish function word.

The KWIC alignment makes it easier to rapidly browse examples, and think about a rough assessment of their word sense or how they are used. Figure 5 compares how the term "God" is used by U.S. presidents Ronald Reagan and Barack Obama, in a corpus of State of the Union speeches, from two different displays of the tool. The predominant usage is the invocation of "God bless America" or similar, nearly ornamental, expressions, but Reagan also has substantive usages, such as references to the role of religion in schools. The vertical alignments of the right-side context words makes it easy to see the "God bless" word sense. I initially found this example simply by browsing the covariate space, and noticing "god" as a frequent term for Reagan, though still occurring for other presidents; the KWIC drilldown better illuminated these distinctions, and suggests differences in political ideologies between the presidents.

In lots of exploratory text analysis work, especially in the topic modeling literature, it is common to look at word lists produced by a statistical analysis method and think about what they might mean. At least in my experience doing this, I've often found that seeing examples of words in context has disproved my initial intuitions. Hopefully, supporting this activity in an interactive user interface might make exploratory analysis more effective. Currently, the interface simply shows a sample of in-context usages from the document query-set; it would be interesting to perform grouping and stratified sampling based on local contextual statistics. Summarizing local context by frequencies could be done as a trie visualization (Wattenberg and Viégas, 2008); see §5.

2.3 Term-association queries

When a term is selected, its interaction with covariates is shown by highlighting documents in (B) that contain the term. This can be thought of as another document query: instead of being specified as a region in the covariate space, is specified as a fragment of the discrete lexical space. As illustrated in much previous work (e.g. Church and Hanks (1990); Turney (2001, 2002)), word-to-word PMI scores can find other terms with similar meanings, or having interesting semantic relationships, to the target term.[2]

This panel ranks terms u by their association with the query term v. The simplest method is to analyze the relative frequencies of terms in documents that contain v,

$$\text{bool-tt-epmi}(u, v) = \frac{p(w_i = u | v \in \text{supp}(d_i))}{p(w_i = u)}$$

Here, the subscript i denotes a token position in the entire corpus, for which there is a wordtype w_i and a document ID d_i. In this notation, the covariate PMI in 2.1 would be $p(w_i = u | d_i \in Q)/p(w_i = u)$. $\text{supp}(d_i)$ denotes the set of terms that occur at least once in document d_i.

This measure is a very simple extension of the document covariate selection mechanism, and easy to understand. However, it is less satisfying for longer documents, since a larger number of occurrences of v do not lead to a stronger association score. A possible extension is to consider the joint random event of selecting two tokens i and j in the corpus, and consider if the two tokens being in the same document is informative for whether the tokens are the words (u, v), i.e.

[2]For finding terms with similar semantic meaning, distributional similarity may be more appropriate (Turney and Pantel, 2010); this could be interesting to incorporate into the software.

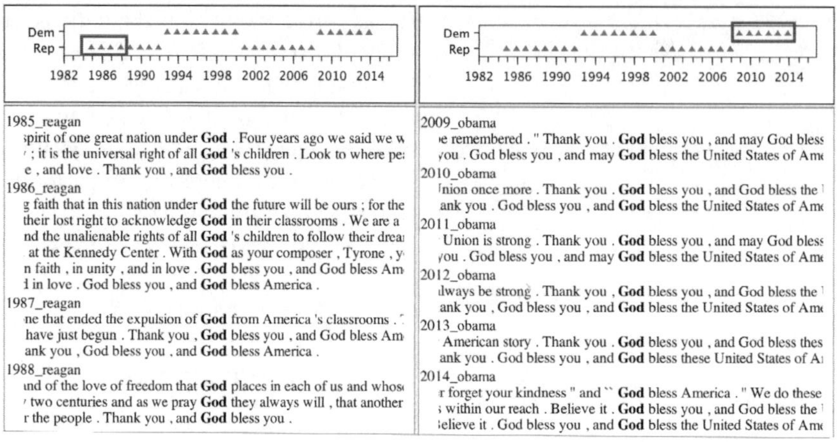

Figure 5: KWIC examples of "God" in speeches by Reagan versus Obama.

$\text{PMI}[(w_i, w_j) = (u, v); d_i = d_j]$,

$$\text{freq-tt-epmi}(u, v) = \frac{p(w_i = u, w_j = v | d_i = d_j)}{p(w_i = u, w_j = v)}$$

In terms of word counts, this expression has the form

$$\text{freq-tt-epmi}(u, v) = \frac{\sum_d n_{du} n_{dv}}{n_u n_v} \frac{N^2}{\sum_d n_d^2}$$

The right-side term is a normalizing constant invariant to u and v. The left-side term is interesting: it can be viewed as a similarity measure, where the numerator is the inner product of the inverted term-document vectors $n_{.,u}$ and $n_{.,v}$, and the denominator is the product of their ℓ_1 norms. This is a very similar form as cosine similarity, which is another normalized inner product, except its denominator is the product of the vectors' ℓ_2 norms.

Term-to-term associations allow a navigation of the term space, complementing the views of terms driven by document covariates. This part of the tool is still at a more preliminary stage of development. One important enhancement would be adjustment of the context window size allowed for co-occurrences; the formulations above assume a context window the size of the document. Medium sized context windows might capture more focused topical content, especially in very long discourses such as speeches; and the smallest context windows, of size 1, should be more like collocation detection (though see §3; this is arguably better done with significance tests, not PMI).

2.4 Pinned terms

The term PMI views of (C) and (D) are very dynamic, which can cause interesting terms to disappear when their supporting query is changed. It is often useful to select terms to be constantly viewed when the document covariate queries change.

Any term can be double-clicked to be moved to the the table of *pinned terms* (B). The set of terms here does not change as the covariate query is changed; a user can fix a set of terms and see how their PMI scores change while looking at different parts of the covariate space. One possible use of term pinning is to manually build up clusters of terms—for example, topical or synonymous term sets—whose aggregate statistical behavior (i.e. as a disjunctive query) may be interesting to observe. Manually built sets of keywords are a very useful form of text analysis; in fact, the WordSeer corpus analysis tool has explicit support to help users create them (Shrikumar, 2013).

3 Statistical term association measures

There exist many measures to measure the statistical strength of an association between a term and a document covariate, or between two terms. A number of methods are based on significance testing, looking for violations of a null hypothesis that term frequencies are independent. For collocation detection, which aims to find meaningful non-compositional lexical items through frequencies of neighboring words, likelihood ratio (Dunning, 1993) and chi-square tests have been used (see review in Manning and Schütze (1999)). For term-covariate associations, chi-square tests were used by Gentzkow and Shapiro (2010) to find politically loaded phrases often used by members of one political party; this same method is often used as a feature selection method for supervised learning (Guyon and Elisseeff, 2003).

The approach we take here is somewhat different, being a point estimate approach, analyzing the estimated difference (and giving poor results when counts are small). Some related work for topic model analysis, looking at statistical associations between words and latent topics (as opposed to between words and observed covariates in this work) includes Chuang et al. (2012b), whose term saliency function measures one word's associations against all topics; a salient term tends to have most of its probability mass in a small set of topics. The measure is a form of mutual information,[3] and may be useful for our purposes here if the user wishes to see a report of distinctive terms for a group of several different observed covariate values at once. Blei and Lafferty (2009) ranks words per topic by a measure inspired by TFIDF, which like PMI downweights words that are generically common across all topics.

Finally, hierarchical priors and regularizers can also be used; for example, by penalizing the log-odds parameterization of term probabilities (Eisenstein et al., 2011; Taddy, 2013). These methods are better in that they incorporate both protection against small count situations, while paying attention to effect size, as well as allowing overlapping covariates and regression control variables; but unfortunately, they are more computationally intensive, as opposed to the above measures which all work directly from sufficient count statistics. An association measure that fulfilled all these desiderata would be very useful. For term-covariate analysis, Monroe et al. (2008) contains a review of many different methods, from both political science as well as computer science; they also propose a hierarchical prior method, and to rank by statistical significance via the asymptotic standard error of the terms' odds ratios.

Given the large amount of previous work using the significance approach, it merits further exploration for this system.

4 Phrase selection

The simplest approach to defining the terms is to use all words (unigrams). This can be insightful, but single words are both too coarse and too narrow a unit of analysis. They can be too narrow when there are multiple ways of saying the same thing, such as synonyms—for example, while we have evidence about differing usages of the term "god" in presidential rhetoric, in order to make a claim about religious themes, we might need to find other terms such as "creator", "higher power", etc. Another problematic case is alternate names or anaphoric references to an entity. In general, any NLP tool that extracts interesting discrete variable indicators of word meaning could be used for mutual information and covariate exploratory analysis—for example, a coreference system's entity ID predictions could be browsed by the system as the term variables. (More complex concepts, of course, would also require more UI support.)

At the same time, words can be too coarse compared to the longer phrases they are contained within, which often contain more interesting and distinctive concepts: for example, "death tax" and "social security" are important concepts in U.S. politics that get missed under a unigram analysis. In fact, Sim et al. (2013)'s analysis of U.S. politicians' speeches found that domain experts had a hard time understanding unigrams out-of-context, but bigrams and trigrams worked much better; Gentzkow and Shapiro (2010) similarly focus on partisan political phrases.

It sometimes works to simply add overlapping n-grams as more terms, but sometimes odd phrases get selected that cross constituent boundaries from their source sentences, and are thus not totally meaningful. I've experimented with a very strong filtering approach to phrase selection: besides using all unigrams, take all n-grams up to length 5 that have nominal part-of-speech patterns: either the sequence consists of zero or more adjectives followed by one or more noun tokens, or all tokens were classified as names by a named entity recognition system.[4] This tends to yield

[3]This is apparent as follows, using notation from their section 3.1:

$$\begin{aligned}\text{saliency}(w) &= p(w)\sum_T p(T|w)\log[p(T|w)/p(T)] \\ &= \sum_T p(w,T)\log[p(w,T)/[p(w)p(T)]]\end{aligned}$$

This might be called a "half-pointwise" mutual information: between a specific word w and the topic random variable T. Mutual information is $\sum_w \text{saliency}(w)$.

[4]For traditional text, the tool currently uses Stanford CoreNLP; for Twitter, CMU ARK TweetNLP.

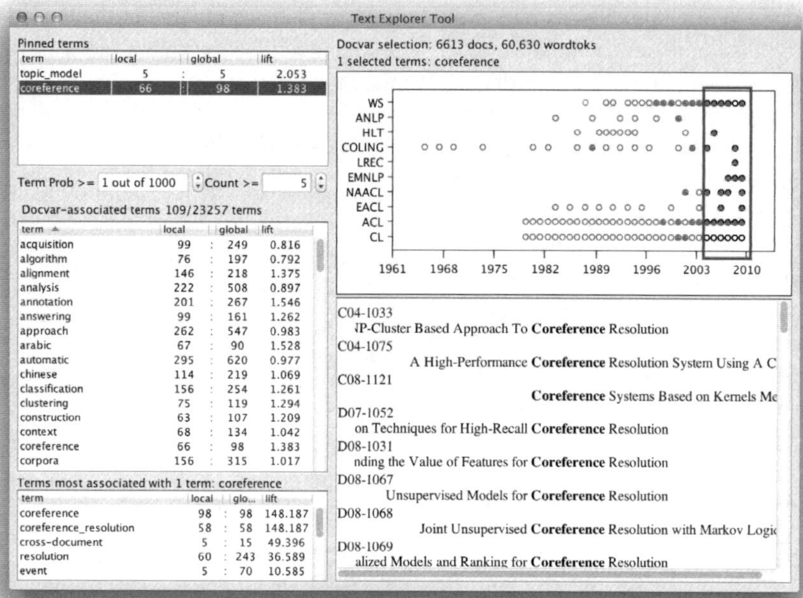

Figure 6: MITEXTEXPLORER for paper titles in the ACL Anthology (Radev et al., 2009). Y-axis is venue (conference or journal name), X-axis is year of publication. Unlike the other figures, docvar-associated terms are sorted alphabetically.

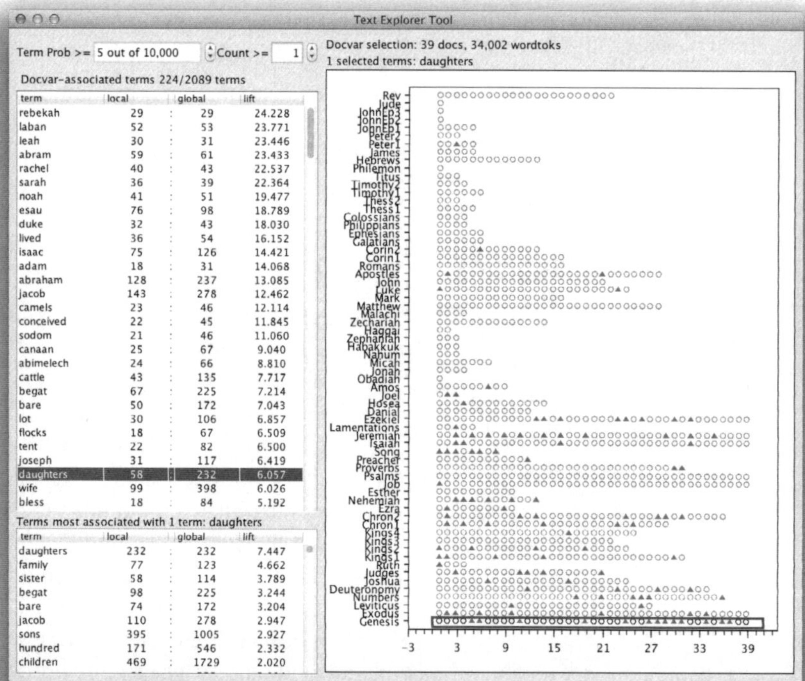

Figure 7: MITEXTEXPLORER for the King James Bible. Y-axis is book, X-axis is chapter (truncated to 39).

(partial) constituents, and nouns tend to be more interesting than other content words (perhaps because they are relatively less reliant on predicate-argument structure to express their semantics—as opposed to adjectives or verbs, say—and a bag-of-terms analysis does not allow expression of argument structure.) However, for many corpora, POS or NER taggers work poorly—for example, I've seen paper titles from the ACL Anthology have capitalized prepositions tagged as names—so simpler stopword heuristics are necessary.

The phrase selection approach could be improved in many ways; for example, a real noun phrase recognizer could get important (NP PP) constructs like "war on terror." Furthermore, Chuang et al. (2012a) find that while these sorts of syntactic features are helpful in choosing useful keyphrases to summarize of scientific abstracts, it is also very useful to add in collocation detection scores. Similarly to the PMI calculations used here, likelihood ratio or chi-square collocation detection statistics are also very rapid to compute and may benefit from interactive adjustment of decision thresholds. More generally, any type of lexicalized linguistic structures could potentially be used, such as dependency paths or constituents from a syntactic parser, or predicate-argument structures from a semantic parser. Linguistic structures extracted from more sophisticated NLP tools may indeed be better-generalized units of linguistic meaning compared to words and phrases, but they will still bear the same high-dimensionality issues for data analysis purposes.

5 Related work: Exploratory text analysis

Many systems and techniques have been developed for interactive text analysis. Two such systems, WordSeer and Jigsaw, have been under development for several years, each having had a series of user experiments and feedback. Recent and interesting review papers and theses are available for both of them.

The WordSeer system (Shrikumar, 2013)[5] contains many different interactive text visualization tools, including syntax-based search, and was initially designed for the needs of text analysis in the humanities; the WordSeer 3.0 system includes a word frequency analysis component that can compare word frequencies along document covariates. Interestingly, Shrikumar found in user studies with literary experts that data comparisons and annotation/note-taking support were very important capabilities to add to the system. Unique to the work in this paper is the emphasis on conditioning on document covariates to analyze relative word frequencies, and encouraging the user to change the statistical parameters that govern text correlation measurements. (The term pinning and term-to-term association techniques are certainly less developed than previous work.)

Another text analysis system is Jigsaw (Görg et al., 2013),[6] originally developed for investigative analysis (as in law enforcement or intelligence), which again has many features. It emphasizes visualizations based on entity extractions, such as for names, places, and dates. Görg et al. note that errors in entity extraction were a major problem for users; this might be a worthwhile argument to focus on getting something to first work with simple words/phrases before tackling more complex units of meaning. A section of the review paper is entitled "Reading the documents still matters", pointing out that analysts did not want just to visualize high-level relationships, but also wanted to read documents in context; this capability was added to later versions of Jigsaw, and supports the emphasis here on the KWIC display.

Both these systems also use variants of Wattenberg and Viégas (2008)'s word tree visualization, which gives a sequential word frequencies as a tree (i.e., what computational linguists might call a trie representation of a high-order Markov model). The "God bless" word sense example from §2 indicates that such statistical summarization of local contextual information may be useful to integrate; it is worth thinking how to integrate this against the important need of document covariate analysis, while being efficient with the use of space.

Many other systems, especially ones designed for literary content analysis, emphasize concordances and keyword searches within a text; for example, Voyeur/Voyant (Rockwell et al., 2010),[7] which also features some document covariate analysis through temporal trend analyses for individual terms. Another class of approaches emphasizes the use of document clustering or topic models (Gardner et al., 2010; Newman et al., 2010;

[5] http://wordseer.berkeley.edu/

[6] http://www.cc.gatech.edu/gvu/ii/jigsaw/

[7] http://voyant-tools.org/, http://hermeneuti.ca/voyeur

Grimmer and King, 2011; Chaney and Blei, 2013), while Overview[8] emphasizes hierarchical document clustering paired with manual tagging.

Finally, considerable research has examined exploratory visual interfaces for information retrieval, in which a user specifies an information need in order to find relevant documents or passages from a corpus (Hearst (2009), Ch. 10). Information retrieval problems have some similarities to text-as-data analysis in the need for an exploratory process of iterative refinement, but the text-as-data perspective differs in that it requires an analyst to understand content and contextual factors across multiple or many documents.

6 Future work

The current MITEXTEXPLORER system is an extremely simple prototype to explore what sorts of "bare words" text-and-covariates analyses are possible. Several major changes will be necessary for more serious use.

First, essential basic capabilities must be added, such as a search box the user can use to search and filter the term list.

Second, the document covariate display needs to support more than just scatterplots. When there are hundreds or more documents, summarization is necessary in the form of histograms, kernel density plots, or other tools. For example, for a large corpus of documents over time, a lineplot or temporal histogram is more appropriate, where each timestep has a document count. The ACL Anthology scatterplot (Figure 6, Radev et al. (2009)), which has hundreds of overplotted points at each (year,venue) position, makes clear the limitations of the current approach.

Better visual feedback for term selections here could be useful—for example, sizing document points monotonically with the term's frequency (rather than just presence/absence), or using stacked line plots—though certain visual depictions of frequency may be difficult given the Zipfian distribution of word frequencies.

Furthermore, document structures may be thought of as document covariates. A single book has interesting internal variation that could be analyzed itself. Figure 7 shows the King James Bible, which has a hierarchical structure of book, chapter, and verse. Here, the (y,x) coordinates represent books and chapters. A more specialized display for book-level structures, or other discourse structures, may be appropriate for book-length texts.

Finally, a major goal of this work is to use analysis methods that can be computed on the fly, but the current prototype only works with small datasets. Hierarchical spatial indexing techniques (e.g. r-trees), may make it possible to interactively compute sums for covariate PMI scoring over very large numbers of documents. Text indexing is also important for term-driven queries and KWIC views. Techniques from ad-hoc data querying systems may be necessary for further scale (e.g. Melnik et al. (2010)).

Many other directions are possible. The prototype tool, as described in §2, will be available as open-source software at: `http://brenocon.com/MiTextExplorer`. It is a desktop application written in Java.

[8]`https://www.overviewproject.org/ http://overview.ap.org/`

Acknowledgments

Thanks to Michael Heilman and Bryan Routledge, for many discussions and creative text analysis scripts that inspired this work. Thanks also to the anonymous reviewers for very helpful feedback. This research was supported in part by NSF grant IIS-1211277 and CAREER grant IIS-1054319.

References

Francis J Anscombe. Graphs in statistical analysis. *The American Statistician*, 27(1):17–21, 1973.

David Bamman, Brendan O'Connor, and Noah A. Smith. Censorship and deletion practices in Chinese social media. *First Monday*, 17(3), 2012.

Richard A Becker and John M Chambers. *S: an interactive environment for data analysis and graphics*. CRC Press, 1984.

Richard A. Becker and William S. Cleveland. Brushing scatterplots. *Technometrics*, 29(2): 127–142, 1987.

David M. Blei and John D. Lafferty. Topic models. *Text mining: classification, clustering, and applications*, 10:71, 2009.

Michael Bostock, Vadim Ogievetsky, and Jeffrey Heer. D3: Data-driven documents. *IEEE Trans. Visualization & Comp. Graphics (Proc. InfoVis)*, 2011. URL `http://vis.stanford.edu/papers/d3`.

Mary Bucholtz, Nancy Bermudez, Victor Fung, Lisa Edwards, and Rosalva Vargas. Hella Nor Cal or totally So Cal? the perceptual dialectology of California. *Journal of English Linguistics*, 35(4):325–352, 2007. URL http://people.duke.edu/~eec10/hellanorcal.pdf.

Andreas Buja, John Alan McDonald, John Michalak, and Werner Stuetzle. Interactive data visualization using focusing and linking. In *Visualization, 1991. Visualization'91, Proceedings., IEEE Conference on*, pages 156–163. IEEE, 1991.

Andreas Buja, Dianne Cook, and Deborah F Swayne. Interactive high-dimensional data visualization. *Journal of Computational and Graphical Statistics*, 5(1):78–99, 1996.

Allison J.B. Chaney and David M. Blei. Visualizing topic models. In *Proceedings of ICWSM*, 2013.

Jason Chuang, Christopher D. Manning, and Jeffrey Heer. "without the clutter of unimportant words": Descriptive keyphrases for text visualization. *ACM Trans. on Computer-Human Interaction*, 19:1–29, 2012a. URL http://vis.stanford.edu/papers/keyphrases.

Jason Chuang, Christopher D. Manning, and Jeffrey Heer. Termite: Visualization techniques for assessing textual topic models. In *Advanced Visual Interfaces*, 2012b. URL http://vis.stanford.edu/papers/termite.

K. W Church and P. Hanks. Word association norms, mutual information, and lexicography. *Computational linguistics*, 16(1):2229, 1990.

William S. Cleveland. *Visualizing data*. Hobart Press, 1993.

Dianne Cook and Deborah F. Swayne. *Interactive and dynamic graphics for data analysis: with R and GGobi*. Springer, 2007.

Ted Dunning. Accurate methods for the statistics of surprise and coincidence. *Computational Linguistics*, 19:61—74, 1993. doi: 10.1.1.14.5962. URL http://citeseerx.ist.psu.edu/viewdoc/summary?doi=10.1.1.14.5962.

J. Eisenstein, A. Ahmed, and E.P. Xing. Sparse additive generative models of text. In *Proceedings of ICML*, pages 1041–1048, 2011.

Jacob Eisenstein, Brendan O'Connor, Noah A. Smith, and Eric P. Xing. A latent variable model for geographic lexical variation. In *Proceedings of the 2010 Conference on Empirical Methods in Natural Language Processing*, pages 1277—1287, 2010.

Jacob Eisenstein, Brendan O'Connor, Noah A. Smith, and Eric P. Xing. Mapping the geographical diffusion of new words. In *NIPS Workshop on Social Network and Social Media Analysis*, 2012. URL http://arxiv.org/abs/1210.5268.

M.J. Gardner, J. Lutes, J. Lund, J. Hansen, D. Walker, E. Ringger, and K. Seppi. The topic browser: An interactive tool for browsing topic models. In *NIPS Workshop on Challenges of Data Visualization. MIT Press*, 2010.

Matthew Gentzkow and Jesse M Shapiro. What drives media slant? evidence from us daily newspapers. *Econometrica*, 78(1):35–71, 2010.

Carsten Görg, Zhicheng Liu, and John Stasko. Reflections on the evolution of the jigsaw visual analytics system. *Information Visualization*, 2013.

Justin Grimmer and Gary King. General purpose computer-assisted clustering and conceptualization. *Proceedings of the National Academy of Sciences*, 108(7):2643–2650, 2011.

Justin Grimmer and Brandon M Stewart. Text as Data: The promise and pitfalls of automatic content analysis methods for political texts. *Political Analysis*, 21(3):267–297, 2013. URL http://www.stanford.edu/~jgrimmer/tad2.pdf.

Isabelle Guyon and André Elisseeff. An introduction to variable and feature selection. *The Journal of Machine Learning Research*, 3:1157–1182, 2003.

Marti Hearst. *Search user interfaces*. Cambridge University Press, 2009.

Matthew L Jockers. *Macroanalysis: Digital methods and literary history*. University of Illinois Press, 2013.

Gary King, Jennifer Pan, and Margaret E. Roberts. How censorship in china allows government criticism but silences collective expression. *American Political Science Review*, 107:1–18, 2013.

Christopher D Manning and Hinrich Schütze. *Foundations of statistical natural language processing*. MIT press, 1999.

Allen R. Martin and Matthew O. Ward. High dimensional brushing for interactive exploration of multivariate data. In *Proceedings of the 6th Conference on Visualization'95*, page 271. IEEE Computer Society, 1995.

Sergey Melnik, Andrey Gubarev, Jing Jing Long, Geoffrey Romer, Shiva Shivakumar, Matt Tolton, and Theo Vassilakis. Dremel: interactive analysis of web-scale datasets. *Proceedings of the VLDB Endowment*, 3(1-2):330–339, 2010.

David Mimno. *Topic regression*. PhD thesis, University of Massachusetts Amherst, 2012.

B. L. Monroe, M. P. Colaresi, and K. M. Quinn. Fightin'Words: lexical feature selection and evaluation for identifying the content of political conflict. *Political Analysis*, 16(4):372, 2008.

D. Newman, T. Baldwin, L. Cavedon, E. Huang, S. Karimi, D. Martinez, F. Scholer, and J. Zobel. Visualizing search results and document collections using topic maps. *Web Semantics: Science, Services and Agents on the World Wide Web*, 8(2):169–175, 2010.

Brendan O'Connor. *Statistical Text Analysis for Social Science*. PhD thesis, Carnegie Mellon University, 2014.

Brendan O'Connor, Michel Krieger, and David Ahn. TweetMotif: Exploratory search and topic summarization for Twitter. In *Proceedings of the International AAAI Conference on Weblogs and Social Media*, 2010.

Brendan O'Connor, David Bamman, and Noah A. Smith. Computational text analysis for social science: Model assumptions and complexity. In *Second Workshop on Comptuational Social Science and the Wisdom of Crowds (NIPS 2011)*, 2011.

Olutobi Owoputi, Brendan O'Connor, Chris Dyer, Kevin Gimpel, Nathan Schneider, and Noah A Smith. Improved part-of-speech tagging for online conversational text with word clusters. In *Proceedings of NAACL*, 2013.

Foster Provost and Tom Fawcett. *Data Science for Business*. O'Reilly Media, 2013.

R Core Team. *R: A Language and Environment for Statistical Computing*. R Foundation for Statistical Computing, Vienna, Austria, 2013. URL `http://www.R-project.org/`. ISBN 3-900051-07-0.

Dragomir R. Radev, Pradeep Muthukrishnan, and Vahed Qazvinian. The ACL anthology network corpus. In *Proc. of ACL Workshop on Natural Language Processing and Information Retrieval for Digital Libraries*, 2009.

Margaret E. Roberts, Brandon M. Stewart, and Edoardo M. Airoldi. Structural topic models. 2013. URL `http://scholar.harvard.edu/bstewart/publications/structural-topic-models`. Working paper.

Geoffrey Rockwell, Stéfan G Sinclair, Stan Ruecker, and Peter Organisciak. Ubiquitous text analysis. *paj: The Journal of the Initiative for Digital Humanities, Media, and Culture*, 2 (1), 2010.

Ryan Shaw. Text-mining as a research tool, 2012. URL `http://aeshin.org/textmining/`.

Aditi Shrikumar. *Designing an Exploratory Text Analysis Tool for Humanities and Social Sciences Research*. PhD thesis, University of California at Berkeley, 2013.

Yanchuan Sim, Brice Acree, Justin H Gross, and Noah A Smith. Measuring ideological proportions in political speeches. In *Proceedings of EMNLP*, 2013.

Matt Taddy. Multinomial inverse regression for text analysis. *Journal of the American Statistical Association*, 108(503):755–770, 2013.

John W. Tukey. *Exploratory data analysis*. 1977.

P. D Turney. Thumbs up or thumbs down?: semantic orientation applied to unsupervised classification of reviews. In *Proceedings of the 40th Annual Meeting on Association for Computational Linguistics*, page 417424, 2002.

P. D Turney and P. Pantel. From frequency to meaning: Vector space models of semantics. *Journal of Artificial Intelligence Research*, 37 (1):141188, 2010. ISSN 1076-9757.

Peter Turney. Mining the web for synonyms: Pmi-ir versus lsa on toefl. In *Proceedings of the Twelth European Conference on Machine Learning*, 2001. URL `http://nparc.cisti-icist.`

nrc-cnrc.gc.ca/npsi/ctrl?action=rtdoc&an=5765594.

Martin Wattenberg and Fernanda B Viégas. The word tree, an interactive visual concordance. *Visualization and Computer Graphics, IEEE Transactions on*, 14(6):1221–1228, 2008.

Hadley Wickham. A layered grammar of graphics. *Journal of Computational and Graphical Statistics*, 19(1):328, 2010. doi: 10.1198/jcgs.2009.07098.

Leland Wilkinson. *The grammar of graphics*. Springer, 2006.

Interactive Learning of Spatial Knowledge for Text to 3D Scene Generation

Angel X. Chang, Manolis Savva and **Christopher D. Manning**
Computer Science Department, Stanford University
{angelx,msavva,manning}@cs.stanford.edu

Abstract

We present an interactive text to 3D scene generation system that learns the expected spatial layout of objects from data. A user provides input natural language text from which we extract explicit constraints on the objects that should appear in the scene. Given these explicit constraints, the system then uses prior observations of spatial arrangements in a database of scenes to infer the most likely layout of the objects in the scene. Through further user interaction, the system gradually adjusts and improves its estimates of where objects should be placed. We present example generated scenes and user interaction scenarios.

1 Introduction

People possess the power of visual imagination that allows them to turn descriptions of scenes into imagery. The conceptual simplicity of generating pictures from descriptions has spurred the desire to make systems capable of this task. However, research into computational systems for creating imagery from textual descriptions has seen only limited success.

Most current 3D scene design systems require the user to learn complex manipulation interfaces through which objects are constructed and precisely positioned within scenes. However, arranging objects in scenes can much more easily be achieved using natural language. For instance, it is much easier to say "Put a cup on the table', rather than having to search for a 3D model of a cup, insert it into the scene, scale it to the correct size, orient it, and position it on a table ensuring it maintains contact with the table. By making 3D scene design more accessible to novice users we empower a broader demographic to create 3D scenes for use cases such as interior design, virtual storyboarding and personalized augmented reality.

Unfortunately, several key technical challenges restrict our ability to create text to 3D scene systems. Natural language is difficult to map to formal representations of spatial knowledge and constraints. Furthermore, language rarely mentions common sense facts about the world, that contain critically important spatial knowledge. For example, people do not usually mention the presence of the ground or that most objects are supported by it. As a consequence, spatial knowledge is severely lacking in current computational systems.

Pioneering work in mapping text to 3D scene representations has taken two approaches to address these challenges. First, by restricting the discourse domain to a micro-world with simple geometric shapes, the SHRDLU system demonstrated parsing of natural language input for manipulating the scene, and learning of procedural knowledge through interaction (Winograd, 1972). However, generalization to scenes with more complex objects and spatial relations is very hard to attain.

More recently, the WordsEye system has focused on the general text to 3D scene generation task (Coyne and Sproat, 2001), allowing a user to generate a 3D scene directly from a textual description of the objects present, their properties and their spatial arrangement. The authors of WordsEye demonstrated the promise of text to scene generation systems but also pointed out some fundamental issues which restrict the success of their system: a lot of spatial knowledge is required which is hard to obtain. As a result, the user has to use unnatural language (e.g. "the stool is 1 feet to the south of the table") to express their intent.

For a text to scene system to understand more natural text, it must be able to infer implicit information not explicitly stated in the text. For instance, given the sentence "there is an office with a red chair", the system should be able to infer

Proceedings of the Workshop on Interactive Language Learning, Visualization, and Interfaces, pages 14–21,
Baltimore, Maryland, USA, June 27, 2014. ©2014 Association for Computational Linguistics

that the office also has a desk in front of the chair. This sort of inference requires a source of prior spatial knowledge. We propose learning this spatial knowledge from existing 3D scene data. However, since the number of available scenes is small, it is difficult to have broad coverage. Therefore, we also rely on user interaction to augment and grow the spatial knowledge. Luckily, user interaction is also natural for scene design since it is an inherently interactive process where user input is needed for refinement.

Our contributions address the fundamental challenges of establishing and interactively expanding a spatial knowledge base. We build on prior work in data-driven scene synthesis (Fisher et al., 2012) to automatically extract general spatial knowledge from data: knowledge of what objects occur in scenes, and their expected spatial relations. Our system then uses this knowledge to generate scenes from natural text inferring implicit constraints. It then leverages user interaction to allow refinement of the scene, and improve the spatial knowledge base. We demonstrate that user interaction is critical in expanding and improving spatial knowledge learned from data.

2 Background

A key insight for enabling text to scene generation is that linguistic and non-linguistic spatial knowledge is critical for this task and can be learned directly from data representing the physical world and from interactions of people with such data. User feedback allows us to interactively update spatial knowledge, an idea that we illustrate here in the domain of spatial relations. Early work on the PUT system (Clay and Wilhelms, 1996) and the SHRDLU system (Winograd, 1972) gives a good formalization of the interactive linguistic manipulation of objects in 3D scenes. Recently, there has been promising work on generating 2D clipart for sentences using probabilistic models with placement priors learned from data (Zitnick et al., 2013).

2.1 Text to Scene Systems

Prior work on text to 3D scene generation has resulted in systems such as WordsEye (Coyne and Sproat, 2001) and other similar approaches (Seversky and Yin, 2006). These systems are typically not designed to be fully interactive and do not leverage user interaction to improve their results. Furthermore, they mostly rely on manual annotation of 3D models and on hand crafted rules to map text to object placement decisions, which makes them hard to extend and generalize. More recent work has used crowdsourcing platforms, such as Amazon Mechanical Turk, to collect necessary annotations (Coyne et al., 2012). However, this data collection is treated as a separate pre-process and the user still has no influence on the system's knowledge base. We address one part of this issue: learning simple spatial knowledge from data and interactively updating it through user feedback. We also infer unstated implicit constraints thus allowing for more natural text input.

2.2 Automatic Scene Layout

Prior work on scene layout has focused largely on room interiors and determining good furniture layouts by optimizing energy functions that capture the quality of a proposed layout. These energy functions are encoded from interior design guidelines (Merrell et al., 2011) or learned from input scene data (Fisher et al., 2012). Knowledge of object co-occurrences and spatial relations is represented by simple models such as mixtures of Gaussians on pairwise object positions and orientations. Methods to learn scene structure have been demonstrated using various data sources including simulation of human agents in 3D scenes (Jiang et al., 2012; Jiang and Saxena, 2013), and analysis of supporting contact points in scanned environments (Rosman and Ramamoorthy, 2011).

However, prior work has not explored methods for enabling users of scene generation algorithms to interactively refine and improve an underlying spatial knowledge model – a capability which is critically important. Our work focuses on demonstrating an interactive system which allows a user to manipulate and refine such spatial knowledge. Such a system is useful regardless of the algorithm used to get the input spatial knowledge.

2.3 Interactive Learning

In many tasks, user interaction can provide feedback to an automated system and guide it towards a desired goal. There is much prior work in various domains including interactive systems for refining image search algorithms (Fogarty et al., 2008) and for manipulating social network group creation (Amershi et al., 2012). We focus on the domain of text to 3D scene generation where despite the success of data-driven methods there has been little work on interactive learning systems.

3 Approach Overview

What should an interactive text to scene system look like from the perspective of a user? The user should be able to provide a brief scene description in natural language as input. The system parses this text to a set of explicitly provided constraints on what objects should be present, and how they are arranged. This set of constraints should be automatically expanded by using prior knowledge so that "common sense" facts are reflected in the general scene – an example is the static support hierarchy for objects in the scene (i.e. plate goes on table, table goes on ground). The system generates a candidate scene and then the user is free to interact with it by direct control or through textual commands. The system can then leverage user interaction to update its spatial knowledge and integrate newly learned constraints or relations. The final output is a 3D scene that can be viewed from any position and rendered by a graphics engine. In this paper we select an initial viewpoint such that objects are in the frame and view-based spatial relations are satisfied.

How might we create such a system? Spatial knowledge is critical for this task. We need it to understand spatial language, to plausibly position objects within scenes and to allow users to manipulate them. We learn spatial knowledge from example scene data to ensure that our approach can be generalized to different scenarios. We also learn from user interaction to refine and expand existing spatial knowledge. In §5 we describe the spatial knowledge used by our system.

We define our problem as the task of taking text describing a scene as input, and generating a plausible 3D scene described by that text as output. More concretely, based on the input text, we select objects from a dataset of 3D models (§4) and arrange them to generate output scenes. See Figure 1 for an illustration of the system architecture. We break the system down into several subtasks:

Constraint Parsing (§6): Parse the input textual description of a concrete scene into a set of constraints on the objects present and spatial relations between them. Automatically expand this set of constraints to account for implicit constraints not specified in the text.

Scene Generation (§7): Using above constraints and prior knowledge on the spatial arrangement of objects, construct a scene template. Next, sample

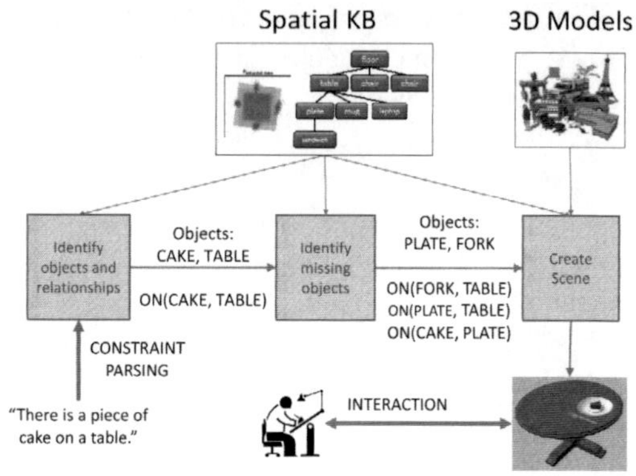

Figure 1: Diagram illustrating the architecture of our system.

the template and select a set of objects to be instantiated. Finally, optimize the placement of the objects to finalize the arrangement of the scene.

Interaction and Learning (§8): Provide means for a user to interactively adjust the scene through direct manipulation and textual commands. Use any such interaction to update the system's spatial knowledge so it better captures the user's intent.

4 Object Knowledge from 3D Models

To generate scenes we need to have a collection of 3D models for representing physical objects. We use a 3D model dataset collected from Google 3D Warehouse by prior work in scene synthesis and containing about 12490 mostly indoor objects (Fisher et al., 2012). These models have text associated with them in the form of names and tags. In addition, we semi-automatically annotated models with object category labels (roughly 270 classes). We used model tags to set these labels, and verified and augmented them manually.

In addition, we automatically rescale models so that they have physically plausible sizes and orient them so that they have a consistent up and front direction (Savva et al., 2014). Due to the number of models in the database, not all models were rescaled and re-oriented. We then indexed all models in a database that we query at run-time for retrieval based on category and tag labels.

5 Spatial Knowledge

Here we describe how we learn spatial knowledge from existing scene data. We base our approach on that of (Fisher et al., 2012) and use their dataset of 133 small indoor scenes created with 1723 3D Warehouse models. Relative object-to-object position and orientation priors can also be learned from the scene data but we have not yet incorporated them in the results for this paper.

5.1 Support Hierarchy

We observe the static support relations of objects in existing scenes to establish a prior over what objects go on top of what other objects. As an example, by observing plates and forks on tables most of the time, we establish that tables are more likely to support plates and forks than chairs. We estimate the probability of a parent category C_p supporting a given child category C_c as a simple conditional probability based on normalized observation counts.

$$P_{support}(C_p|C_c) = \frac{count(C_c \text{ on } C_p)}{count(C_c)}$$

5.2 Supporting surfaces

To identify which surfaces on parent objects support child objects, we first segment parent models into planar surfaces using a simple region-growing algorithm based on (Kalvin and Taylor, 1996). We characterize support surfaces by the direction of their normal vector limited to the six canonical directions: *up, down, left, right, front, back.* We then learn a probability of supporting surface normal direction S_n given child object category C_c. For example, posters are typically found on walls so their support normal vectors are in the horizontal directions. Any unobserved child categories are assumed to have $P_{surf}(S_n = up|C_c) = 1$ since most things rest on a horizontal surface (e.g. floor).

$$P_{surf}(S_n|C_c) = \frac{count(C_c \text{ on surface with } S_n)}{count(C_c)}$$

5.3 Spatial Relations

For spatial relations we use a set of predefined relations: *left, right, above, below, front, back, on top of, next to, near, inside, and outside*. These are measured using axis-aligned bounding boxes from the viewer's perspective. More concretely, the bounding boxes of the two objects involved in a spatial relation are compared to determine volume overlap or closest distance (for proximity relations). Table 1 gives a few examples of the definitions of these spatial relations.

Since these spatial relations are resolved with respect to the current view of the scene, they correspond to view-centric definitions of these spatial concepts. An interesting line of future work would be to explore when ego-centric and object-centric spatial reference models are more likely in a given utterance, and resolve the spatial term accordingly.

Relation	$P(relation)$
inside(A,B)	$\frac{Vol(A \cap B)}{Vol(A)}$
outside(A,B)	$1 - \frac{Vol(A \cap B)}{Vol(A)}$
left(A,B)	$\frac{Vol(A \cap \text{left}(B))}{Vol(A)}$
right(A,B)	$\frac{Vol(A \cap \text{right}(B))}{Vol(A)}$
near(A,B)	$\mathbb{1}(dist(A,B) < t_{near})$

Table 1: Definitions of spatial relation using object bounding box computations. Note that $dist(A, B)$ is normalized with respect to the maximum extent of the bounding box of B.

6 Constraint Parsing

During constraint parsing we take the input text and identify the objects and the relations between them. For each object, we also identify properties associated with it such as category label, basic attributes such as color and material, and number of occurrences in the scene. Based on the object category and attributes, and other words in the noun phrase mentioning the object, we identify a set of associated keywords to be used later for querying the 3D model database. Spatial relations between objects are extracted as predicates of the form *on(A,B)* or *left(A,B)* where *A* and *B* are recognized objects.

As an example, given the input "There is a room with a desk and a red chair. The chair is to the left of the desk." we extract the following objects and spatial relations:

Objects:

index	category	attributes	keywords
0	room		room
1	desk		desk
2	chair	*color*:red	chair, red

Relations: left(chair, desk)

The input text is processed using the Stanford CoreNLP pipeline[1]. We use the Stanford coreference system to determine when the same object is being referred to. To identify objects, we look for noun phrases and use the head word as the category, filtering with WordNet (Miller, 1995) to determine which objects are visualizable (under the

[1] http://nlp.stanford.edu/software/corenlp.shtml

Dependency Pattern	*Example Text*
`tag:VBN=verb >nsubjpass =nsubj >prep (=prep >pobj =pobj)`	The chair$_{[nsubj]}$ is made$_{[verb]}$ of$_{[prep]}$ wood$_{[pobj]}$
`tag:VB=verb >dobj =dobj >prep (=prep >pobj =pobj)`	Put$_{[verb]}$ the cup$_{[dobj]}$ on$_{[prep]}$ the table$_{[pobj]}$

Table 2: Example dependency patterns for extracting spatial relations.

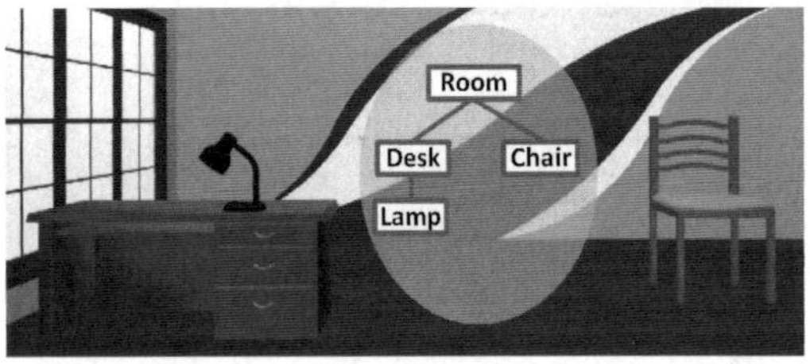

Figure 2: Generated scene for "There is a room with a desk and a lamp. There is a chair to the right of the desk." The inferred scene hierarchy is overlayed in the center.

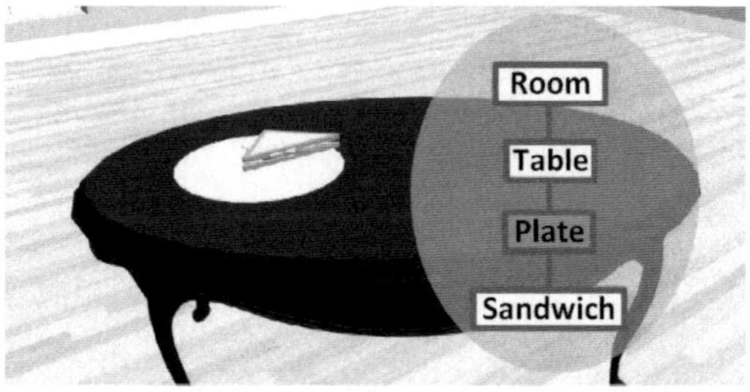

Figure 4: Generated scene for "There is a room with a table and a sandwich." Note that the plate is not explicitly stated, but is inferred by the system.

physical object synset, excluding locations). To identify properties of the objects, we extract other adjectives and nouns in the noun phrase. We also match dependency patterns such as "X is made of Y" to extract more attributes and keywords. Finally, we use dependency patterns to extract spatial relations between objects (see Table 2 for some example patterns).

We used a fairly simple deterministic approach to map text to the scene template and user actions on the scene. An interesting avenue for future research is to automatically learn how to map text using more advanced semantic parsing methods.

7 Scene Generation

During scene generation we aim to find the most likely scene given the input utterance, and prior knowledge. Once we have determined from the input text what objects exist and their spatial relations in the scene, we select 3D models matching the objects and their associated properties. We sample the support hierarchy prior $P_{support}$ to obtain the support hierarchy for the scene.

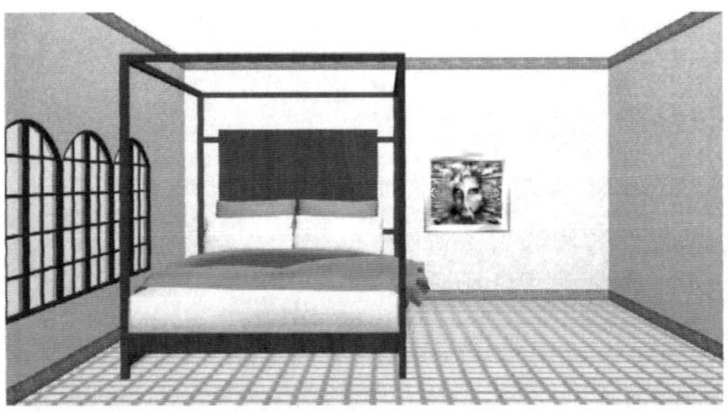

Figure 3: Generated scene for "There is a room with a poster bed and a poster."

We then initialize the positions of objects within the scene by traversing the support hierarchy in depth-first order, positioning the largest available child node and recursing. Child nodes are positioned by selecting a supporting surface on a candidate parent object through sampling of P_{surf} and ensuring no collisions exist with other objects. If there are any spatial constraints that are not satisfied, we remove and randomly reposition the objects violating the constraints, and iterate to improve the layout. The resulting scene is rendered and presented to the user.

Figure 2 shows a rendering of a generated scene along with the support hierarchy and input text. Even though the spatial relation between lamp and desk was not mentioned explicitly, we infer that the lamp is supported by the top surface of the desk. In Figure 3 we show another example of a generated scene for the input "There is a room with a poster bed and a poster". Note that the system differentiates between a "poster" and a "poster bed" – it correctly selects and places the bed on the floor, while the poster is placed on the wall.

Figure 4 shows an example of inferring missing objects. Even though the plate was not explicitly mentioned in the input, we infer that the sandwich is more likely to be supported by a plate rather than directly placed on the table. Without this infer-

Figure 5: **Left**: chair is selected using "the chair to the right of the table" or "the object to the right of the table". Chair is not selected for "the cup to the right of the table". **Right**: Different view results in different chair being selected for the input "the chair to the right of the table".

ence, the user would need to be much more verbose with text such as "There is a room with a table, a plate and a sandwich. The sandwich is on the plate, and the plate is on the table."

8 Interactive System

Once a scene is generated, the user can view the scene and manipulate it using both simple action phrases and mouse interaction. The system supports traditional 3D scene interaction mechanisms such as navigating the viewpoint with mouse and keyboard, selection and movement of object models by clicking. In addition, a user can give simple textual commands to select and modify objects, or to refine the scene. For example, a user can request to "remove the chair" or "put a pot on the table" which requires the system to resolve referents to objects in the scene (see §8.1). The system tracks user interactions throughout this process and can adjust its spatial knowledge accordingly. In the following sections, we give some examples of how the user can interact with the system and how the system learns from this interaction.

8.1 View centric spatial relations

During interaction, the user can refer to objects with their categories and with spatial relations between them. Objects are disambiguated by both category and view-centric spatial relations. We use the WordNet hierarchy to resolve hyponym or hypernym referents to objects in the scene. In the left screenshot in Figure 5, the user can select a chair to the right of the table using the phrase "chair to the right of the table" or "object to the right of the table". The user can then change their viewpoint by rotating and moving around. Since spatial relations are resolved with respect to the current viewpoint, we see that a different chair is selected for the same phrase from the different viewpoint in the right screenshot.

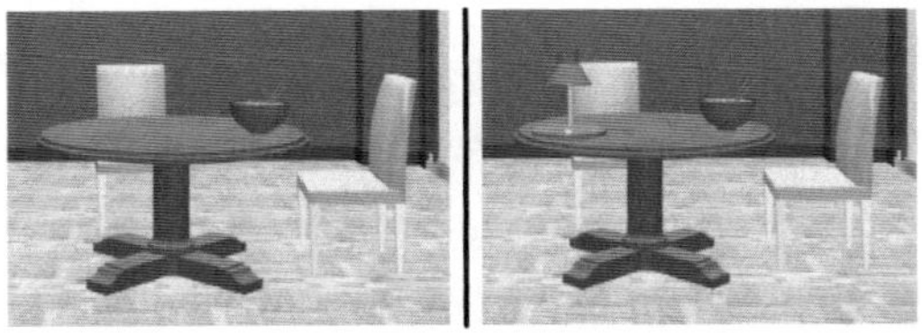

Figure 6: **Left**: initial scene. **Right**: after input "Put a lamp on the table".

8.2 Scene Editing with Text

By using simple textual commands the user can edit the scene. For example, given the initial scene on the left in Figure 6, the user can then issue the command "put a lamp on the table" which results in the scene on the right. The system currently allows for adding objects to new positions and removing existing objects. Currently, repositioning of objects is performed only with direct control, but in the future we also plan to support repositioning of objects by using textual commands.

8.3 Learning Support Hierarchy

After a user requests that a lamp be placed on a table, the system updates its prior on the likelihood of a lamp being supported by a table. Based on prior observations the likelihood of lamps being placed on tables was very low (4%) since very few lamps were observed on tables in the scene dataset. However, after the user interaction, we recompute the prior including the scene that the user has created and the probability of lamp on table increases to 12% (see Figure 7).

8.4 Learning Object Names

Often, objects or parts may not have associated labels that the user would use to refer to the objects. In those cases, the system can inform the user that it cannot resolve a given name, and the user can then select the object or part of the object they were referring to and annotate it with a label. For instance, in Figure 8, the user annotated the different parts of the room as "floor", "wall", "window", and "door". Before annotation, the system did not know any labels for these parts of the room. After annotation, the user can select these parts using the associated names. In addition, the system updates its spatial knowledge base and can now predict that the probability of a poster being placed on a wall

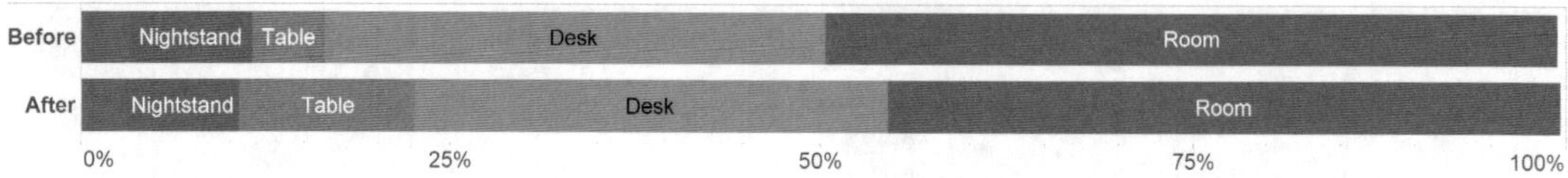

Figure 7: Probability of supporting parent categories for lamps before and after the user explicitly requests a lamp on a table.

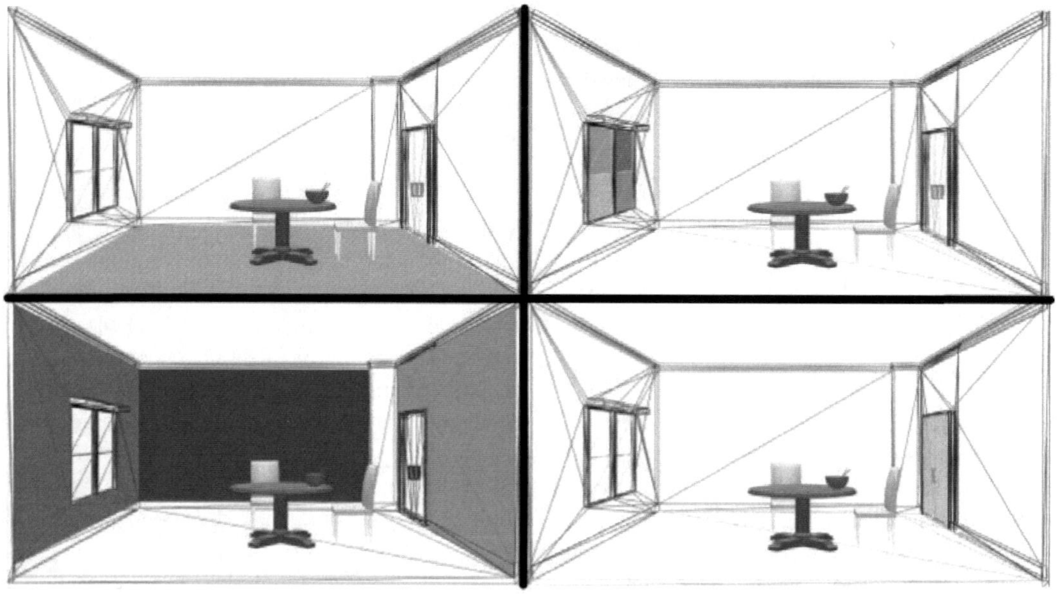

Figure 8: The user clicks and selects parts of the scene, annotating them as "floor", "wall", "window", "door". After annotation, the user can also refer to these parts with the associated names. The system spatial knowledge base is updated accordingly.

is 40%, and that the probability of a table being placed on the floor is 23%. Note that these probabilities are based on multiple observations of the annotated room. Accumulating annotations such as these and propagating labels to new models is an effective way to expand spatial knowledge.

9 Future Work

We described a preliminary interactive text to 3D scene generation system that can learn from prior data and user interaction. We hope to improve the system by incorporating more feedback mechanisms for the user, and the learning algorithm.

If the user requests a particular object be selected but the system gets the referent wrong, the user could then indicate the error and provide a correction. We can then use this feedback as a source of training data to improve the interpretation of text to the desired user action. For example, if the user asks to "select the red bowl" and the system could not resolve "red bowl" to the correct object, the user could intervene by clicking on the correct referent object. Simple interactions such as this are incredibly powerful for providing additional data for learning. Though we did not focus on this aspect, a dialogue-based interaction pattern is natural for our system. The user can converse with the system to iteratively refine the scene and the system can ask for clarifications at any point – when and how the system should inquire for more information is interesting future research.

To evaluate whether the generated scenes are satisfactory, we can ask people to rate them against input text descriptions. We can also study usage of the system in concrete tasks to see how often users need to provide corrections and manually manipulate the scene. A useful baseline to compare against would be a traditional scene manipulation system. By doing these studies at a large scale, for instance by making the interface available on the web, we can crowdsource the accumulation of user interactions and gathering of spatial knowledge. Simultaneously, running formal user studies to better understand preference for text-based versus direct interactions during different actions would be very beneficial for more informed design of text-to-scene generation systems.

10 Conclusion

We have demonstrated the usefulness of an interactive text to 3D scene generation system. Spatial knowledge is essential for text to 3D scene generation. While it is possible to learn spatial knowledge purely from data, it is hard to have complete coverage of all possible scenarios. Interaction and user feedback is a good way to improve coverage and to refine spatial knowledge. In addition, interaction is a natural mode of user involvement in scene generation and creative tasks.

Little prior work has addressed the need for interaction or the need for recovering implicit spatial constraints. We propose that the resolution of unmentioned spatial constraints, and leveraging user interaction to acquire spatial knowledge are critical for enabling natural text to scene generation.

User interaction is essential for text to scene generation since the process is fundamentally under-constrained. Most natural textual descriptions of scenes will not mention many visual aspects of a physical scene. However, it is still possible to automatically generate a plausible starting scene for refinement.

Our work focused on showing that user interaction is both natural and useful for a text to scene generation system. Furthermore, refining spatial knowledge through interaction is a promising way of acquiring more implicit knowledge. Finally, any practically useful text to scene generation will by necessity involve interaction with users who have particular goals and tasks in mind.

References

Saleema Amershi, James Fogarty, and Daniel Weld. 2012. Regroup: interactive machine learning for on-demand group creation in social networks. In *Proceedings of the SIGCHI Conference on Human Factors in Computing Systems*.

Sharon Rose Clay and Jane Wilhelms. 1996. Put: Language-based interactive manipulation of objects. *Computer Graphics and Applications, IEEE*.

Bob Coyne and Richard Sproat. 2001. WordsEye: an automatic text-to-scene conversion system. In *Proceedings of the 28th annual conference on Computer graphics and interactive techniques*.

Bob Coyne, Alexander Klapheke, Masoud Rouhizadeh, Richard Sproat, and Daniel Bauer. 2012. Annotation tools and knowledge representation for a text-to-scene system. *Proceedings of COLING 2012: Technical Papers*.

Matthew Fisher, Daniel Ritchie, Manolis Savva, Thomas Funkhouser, and Pat Hanrahan. 2012. Example-based synthesis of 3D object arrangements. *ACM Transactions on Graphics (TOG)*.

James Fogarty, Desney Tan, Ashish Kapoor, and Simon Winder. 2008. CueFlik: interactive concept learning in image search. In *Proceedings of the SIGCHI Conference on Human Factors in Computing Systems*.

Yun Jiang and Ashutosh Saxena. 2013. Infinite latent conditional random fields for modeling environments through humans.

Yun Jiang, Marcus Lim, and Ashutosh Saxena. 2012. Learning object arrangements in 3D scenes using human context. In *Proceedings of the 29th International Conference on Machine Learning (ICML-12)*.

Alan D Kalvin and Russell H Taylor. 1996. Superfaces: Polygonal mesh simplification with bounded error. *Computer Graphics and Applications, IEEE*.

Paul Merrell, Eric Schkufza, Zeyang Li, Maneesh Agrawala, and Vladlen Koltun. 2011. Interactive furniture layout using interior design guidelines. In *ACM Transactions on Graphics (TOG)*.

G.A. Miller. 1995. WordNet: a lexical database for english. *CACM*.

Benjamin Rosman and Subramanian Ramamoorthy. 2011. Learning spatial relationships between objects. *The International Journal of Robotics Research*.

Manolis Savva, Angel X. Chang, Gilbert Bernstein, Christopher D. Manning, and Pat Hanrahan. 2014. On being the right scale: Sizing large collections of 3D models. *Stanford University Technical Report CSTR 2014-03*.

Lee M Seversky and Lijun Yin. 2006. Real-time automatic 3D scene generation from natural language voice and text descriptions. In *Proceedings of the 14th annual ACM international conference on Multimedia*.

Terry Winograd. 1972. Understanding natural language. *Cognitive psychology*.

C Lawrence Zitnick, Devi Parikh, and Lucy Vanderwende. 2013. Learning the visual interpretation of sentences. In *IEEE Intenational Conference on Computer Vision (ICCV)*.

Dynamic Wordclouds and Vennclouds for Exploratory Data Analysis

Glen Coppersmith
Human Language Technology Center of Excellence
Johns Hopkins University
coppersmith@jhu.edu

Erin Kelly
Department of Defense
elkelly8@gmail.com

Abstract

The *wordcloud* is a ubiquitous visualization of human language, though it falls short when used for exploratory data analysis. To address some of these shortcomings, we give the viewer explicit control over the creation of the wordcloud, allowing them to interact with it in real time– a *dynamic wordcloud*. This allows iterative adaptation of the visualization to the data and inference task at hand. We next present a principled approach to visualization which highlights the similarities and differences between two sets of documents – a *Venncloud*. We make all the visualization code (primarily JavaScript) freely available.

1 Introduction

A cornerstone of exploratory data analysis is visualization. Tremendous academic effort and engineering expertise has created and refined a myriad of visualizations available to the data explorer, yet there still exists a paucity of options for visualizing language data. While *visualizing human language* is a broad subject, we apply Polya's dictum, and examine a pair of simpler questions for which we still lack an answer:

- **(1) what is in this corpus of documents?**
- **(2) what is the relationship between these two corpora of documents?**

We assert that addressing these two questions is a step towards creating visualizations of human language more suitable for exploratory data analysis. In order to create a meaningful visualization, one must understand the inference question the visualization is meant to inform (i.e., the reason for which **(1)** is being asked), so the appropriate aspects of the data can be highlighted with the aesthetics of the visualization. Different inference questions require different aspects to be highlighted, so we aim to create a maximally-flexible, yet simple and intuitive method to enable a user to explore the relevant aspects of their data, and adapt the visualization to their task at hand.

The primary contributions of this paper are:

- A visualization of language data tailored for exploratory data analysis, designed to examine a single corpus (the *dynamic wordcloud*) and to compare two corpora (the *Venncloud*);
- The framing and analysis of the problem in terms of the existing psychophysical literature;
- Distributable JavaScript code, designed to be simple to use, adapt, and extend.

We base our visualizations on the wordcloud, which we deconstruct and analyze in §3 and §4. We then discuss the literature on wordclouds and relevant psychophysical findings in §5, taking guidance from the practical and theoretical foundations explored there. We then draw heavily on similarities to more common and well understood visualizations to create a more useful version of the wordcloud. Question **(1)** is addressed in §7, and with only a small further expansion described in §8, an approach to **(2)** becomes evident.

2 Motivating Inference Tasks

Exploratory data analysis on human language encompasses a diverse set of language and inference tasks, so we select the following subset for their variety. One task in line with question **(1)** is getting the general subject of a corpus, highlighting content-bearing words. One might want to examine a collection of social media missives, too numerous to read individually, perhaps to detect emerging news (Petrovic et al., 2013). Separately, author identification (or idiolect analysis)

Proceedings of the Workshop on Interactive Language Learning, Visualization, and Interfaces, pages 22–29,
Baltimore, Maryland, USA, June 27, 2014. ©2014 Association for Computational Linguistics

attempts attribution of documents (e.g., Shakespeare's plays or the Federalist papers) by comparing the author's writing style, focusing on stylistic and content*less* words – for a review see (Juola, 2006). Further, some linguistic psychometric analysis depends on the relative distribution of pronouns and other seemingly contentless words (Coppersmith et al., 2014a; Chung and Pennebaker, 2007).

Each of these questions involves some analysis of unigram statistics, but exactly what analysis differs significantly, thus no single wordcloud can display all of them. Any static wordcloud is a single point in a distribution of possible wordclouds – one way of calculating statistics from the underlying language and mapping those calculations to the visual representation. Many such combinations and mappings are available, and the optimal wordcloud, like the optimal plot, is a function of the data and the inference task at hand. Thus, we enable the wordcloud viewer to adjust the relationship between the aspects of the data and the aesthetics of the display, which allows them to view different points in the distribution of possible wordclouds. The dynamic wordcloud was implicitly called for in (Rayson and Garside, 2000) since human expertise (specifically knowledge of broader contexts and common sense) is needed to separate meaningful and non-meaningful differences in wordclouds. We enable this dynamic interaction between human and visualization in real-time with a simple user interface, requiring only a modicum more engineering than the creation of a static wordcloud, though the depth of extra information conveyed is significant.

3 Wordcloud Aesthetics

We refer to each visual component of the visualization as an *aesthetic* (ala (Wickham, 2009)) – each aesthetic can convey some information to the viewer. For context, the aesthetics of a scatterplot include the x and y position, color, and size of each point. Some are best suited for ordinal data (e.g., font size), while others for categorical data (e.g., font color).

Ordinal data can be encoded by font size, the most prominent and noticeable to the viewer (Bateman et al., 2008). Likewise, the opacity (transparency) of the word is a prominent and ordinal aesthetic. The order in which words are displayed can convey a significant amount of information as well, but using order in this fashion generally constrains the use of x and y position.

Categorical data can be encoded by the color of each word – both the foreground of the word itself and the background space that surrounds it (though that bandwidth is severely limited by human perception). Likewise for font weight (boldness) and font decoration (italics and underlines). While font face itself could encode a categorical variable, making comparisons of all the other aspects across font faces is likely to be at best uninformative and at worst misleading.

4 Data Aspects

As the wordcloud has visual *aesthetics* that we can control (§3), the data we need to model has *aspects* that we want to represent with those aesthetics. This aspect-to-aesthetic mapping is what makes a useful and informative visualization, and needs to be flexible enough to allow it be used for a range of inference tasks.

For clarity, we define a *word* (w) as a unique set of characters and a *word token* ($\mathbf{w}$) as a single usage of a word in a document. We can observe multiple word tokens ($\mathbf{w}$) of the same word (w) in a single document (d). For any document d we represent the term frequency of w as $tf_d(w)$. Similarly, the inverse document frequency of w as $idf(w)$. A combination of tf and idf is often used to determine important words in a document or corpus. We focus on tf and idf here, but this is just an example of an ordinal value associated with a word, there are many other such word-ordinal pairings that are worth exploring (e.g., weights in a classifier).

The dynamic range ("scaling" in (Wickham, 2009)) also needs to be considered, since the data has a natural dynamic range – where meaningful differences can be observed (unsurprisingly, the definition of *meaningful* depends on the inference task). Likewise, each aesthetic has a range of values for which the users can perceive and differentiate (e.g., words in a font size too small are illegible, those too large prevent other words from being displayed; not all differences are perceptible). Mapping the relevant dynamic range of the data to the dynamic range of the visualization is at the heart of a good visualization, but to do this algorithmically for all possible inference tasks remains a challenge. We, instead, enable the user to adjust the dynamic range of the visualization explicitly.

5 Prior Art

Wordclouds have a mixed history, stemming from Jim Flanagan's "Search Referral Zeitgeist", used to display aggregate information about websites linking to his, to its adoption as a visual gimmick, to the paradoxical claim that 'wordclouds work in practice, but not in theory' (see (Viégas and Wattenberg, 2008) for more). A number of wordcloud-generators exist on the web (e.g., (Feinberg, 2013; Davies, 2013)), though these tend towards creating art rather than informative visualizations. The two cited do allow the user limited interaction with some of the visual aesthetics, though not of sufficient scope or response time for general exploratory data analysis.

Enumerating all possible inference tasks involving the visualization of natural language is impossible, but the prior art does provide empirical data for some relevant tasks. This further stresses the importance of allowing the user to interact with the visualization, since optimizing the visualization *a priori* for all inference tasks simultaneously is not possible, much like creating a single plot for all numerical inference tasks is not possible.

5.1 Psychophysical Analyses

The quintessential studies on how a wordcloud is interpreted by humans can be found in (Rivadeneira et al., 2007) and (Bateman et al., 2008). They both investigated various measures of impression-forming and recall to determine which aesthetics conveyed information most effectively – font size chief among them.

Rivandeneira et al. (Rivadeneira et al., 2007) also found that word-order was important for impression forming (displaying words from most frequent to least frequent was most effective here), while displaying words alphabetically was best when searching for a known word. They also found that users prefer a search box when searching for something specific and known, and a wordcloud for exploratory tasks and things unknown.

Bateman et al. (Bateman et al., 2008) examined the relative utility of other aesthetics to convey information, finding that font-weight (boldness) and intensity (opacity) are effective, but not as good as font-size. Aesthetics such as color, number of characters or the area covered by the word were less effective.

Significant research has gone in to the placement of words in the wordcloud (e.g., (Seifert et al., 2008)), though seemingly little information can be conveyed by these layouts (Schrammel et al., 2009). Indeed, (Rivadeneira et al., 2007) indicates that words directly adjacent to the largest word in the wordcloud had slightly worse recall than those not-directly-adjacent – in essence, getting the most important words in the center may be counterproductive. Thus we eschew these algorithms in favor of more interpretable (but perhaps less aesthetically pleasing) linear ordered layouts.

5.2 Wordclouds as a tool

Illustrative investigations of the wordcloud as a tool for exploratory data analysis are few, but encouraging.

In relation to question **(1)**, even static wordclouds can be useful for this task. Users performing an open-ended search task preferred using a wordcloud to a search box (Sinclair and Cardew-Hall, 2008), possibly because the wordcloud prevented them from having to hypothesize what might be in the collection before searching for it. Similarly, wordclouds can be used as a follow-up display of search results from a query performed via a standard text search box (Knautz et al., 2010), providing the user a crude summary of the results. In both of these cases, a simple static wordcloud is able to provide some useful information to the user, though less research has been done to determine the optimal composition of the wordcloud. What's more, the need for a dynamic interactive wordcloud was made explicit (Knautz et al., 2010), given the way the users iteratively refined their queries and wordclouds.

Question **(2)** has also been examined. One approach is to make a set of wordclouds with soft constraints that the same word appears in roughly the same position across multiple clouds to facilitate comparisons (Castella and Sutton, 2013). Each of these clouds in a *wordstorm* visualizes a different collection of documents (e.g., subdivisions via metadata of a larger corpus).

Similarly addressing our second question, Parallel Tag Clouds (Collins et al., 2009) allow the comparison of multiple sets of documents (or different partitions of a corpus). This investigation provides a theoretically-justified approach to finding 'the right' static wordcloud (for a single inference task), though this does depend on some language-specific resources (e.g., stopword lists and stemming). Interestingly, they opt for explicit removal of words and outliers that the user does not wish to have displayed (an exclusion list), rather than adjusting calculations of the entire cloud to remove them in a principled and fair manner.

5.3 Wordclouds and Metadata

Wordclouds have previously been extended to convey additional information, though these adaptations have been optimized generally for artistic purposes rather than exploratory data analysis.

Wordclouds can been used to display how language interacts with a temporal dimension in (Dubinko et al., 2007; Cui et al., 2010; Lee et al., 2010). Dubinko and colleagues created a tag cloud variant that displays trends in tag usage over time, coupled with images that have that tag (Dubinko et al., 2007). An information-theoretic approach to displaying information changing in time gives rise to a theoretically grounded approach for displaying pointwise tag clouds, and highlighting those pieces that have changed significantly as compared to a previous time period (Cui et al., 2010). This can be viewed as measuring the change in overall language usage over time. In contrast, using spark lines on each individual word or tag can convey temporal trends for individual words (Lee et al., 2010).

Meanwhile, combining tag clouds with geospatial data yields a visualization where words can be displayed on a map of the world in locations they are frequently tagged in, labeling famous landmarks, for example (Slingsby et al., 2007).

6 Desiderata

In light of the diverse inference tasks (§2) and prior art (§5), the following desiderata emerge for the visualization. These desiderata are explicit choices, not all of which are ideal for all inference tasks. Thus, chief among them is the first: flexibility to allow maximum extensions and modifications as needed.

Flexible and **adjustable in real time**: Any single static wordcloud is guaranteed to be suboptimal for at least some inference tasks, so allowing the user to adjust the aspect-to-aesthetic mapping of the wordcloud in real time enables adaptation of the visualization to the data and inference task at hand. The statistics described in §4 are relevant to every language collection (and most inference tasks), yet there are a number of other ordinal values to associate a word (e.g., the weight assigned to it by a classifier). Thus, tf and idf are meant to be illustrative examples though the visualization code should generalize well to others.

Though removal of the most frequent words (stopwords) is useful in many natural language processing tasks, there are many ways to define which words fall under this category. Unsurprisingly, the optimal selection of these words can also depend upon the task at hand (e.g., psychiatric v. thematic analysis as in §2), so maximum flexibility and minimum latency are desirable.

Interpretable: An explicit legend is needed to interpret the differences in visual aesthetics and what these differences mean with respect to the underlying data aspects.

Language-Agnostic: We need methods for exploratory data analysis that work well regardless of the language(s) being investigated. This is crucial for multilingual corpora, yet decidedly nontrivial. These techniques must be maximally language-agnostic, relying on only the most rudimentary understanding of the linguistic structure of the data (e.g., spaces separate words in English, but not in Chinese), so they can be extended to many languages easily.

This precludes the use of a fixed set of stop words for each language examined, since a new set of stopwords would be required for each language explored. Alternatively, the set of stopwords can be dealt with automatically, either by granting the user the ability to filter out words in the extremes of the distributions (tf and df alike) through the use of a weight which penalizes these ubiquitous or too-rare words. Similarly precluded is the use of stemming to deal with the many surface forms of a given root word (e.g., type, typing, typed).

7 Dynamic Wordclouds

We address Question **(1)** and a number of our desiderata with the addition of explicitly labeled controls to the static wordcloud display, which allows the user to control the mapping from data aspects to the visualization aesthetics. We supplement these controls with an explicit explanation of how each aesthetic is affected by each aspect, so the user can easily read the relevant mappings, rather than trying to interpret the location of the sliders. An example of which is that "Larger words are those that frequently occur in the query", when the aspect tf is mapped to the

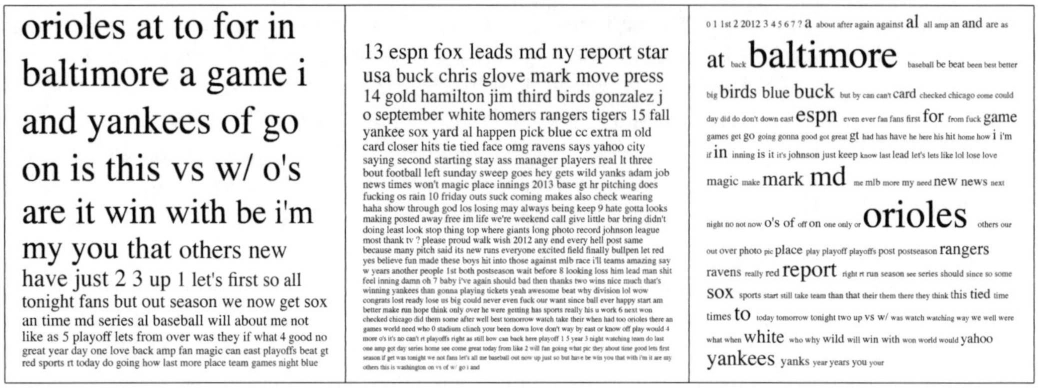

Figure 1: Three example settings of the dynamic wordcloud for the same set of tweets containing "Orioles". Left: size reflects tf, sorted by tf; Center: size reflects idf, sorted by idf; Right: size reflects tf*idf, sorted alphabetically.

aesthetic font-size (and this description is tied to the appropriate sliders so it updates as the sliders are changed). The manipulation of the visualization in real time allows us to take advantage of the human's adept visual change-detection to highlight and convey the differences between settings (or a range of settings), even subtle ones.

The data aspects from §4 are precomputed and mapped to the aesthetics from §3 in a JavaScript visualization displayed in a standard web browser. This visualization enables the user to manipulate the aspect-to-aesthetic mapping via an intuitive set of sliders and buttons, responsive in real time. The sliders are roughly segmented into three categories: those that control which words are displayed, those that control how size is calculated, and those that control how opacity is calculated. The buttons control the order in which words appear.

One set of sliders controls which words are displayed by examining the frequency and rarity of the words. We define the range $\tau_{Freq} = [t^{min}_{Freq}, t^{max}_{Freq}]$ as the range of tf values for words to be displayed (i.e., $tf(w) \in \tau_{Freq}$). The viewer is granted a range slider to manipulate both t^{min}_{Freq} and t^{max}_{Freq} to eliminate words from the extremes of the distribution. Similarly for df and τ_{Rarity}. Those words that fall outside τ_{Freq} or τ_{Rarity} are not displayed. Importantly, tf is computed from the current corpus displayed while df is computed over a much larger collection (in our running examples, all the works of Shakespeare or all the tweets for the last 6 months). Those with high df or high tf are often stopwords, those with low tf and low df are often rare, sometimes too rare to get good estimates of tf or idf (e.g., names).

A second set of sliders controls the mapping between aspects and aesthetics for each individual word. Each aesthetic has a weight for the importance of rarity (γ_{Rarity}) and the importance of frequency (γ_{Freq}), corresponding to the current values of their respective slider (each in the range $[0, 1]$). For size, we compute a weight attributed to each data aspect:

$$\omega_{Freq}(w) = (1 - \gamma_{Freq}) + \gamma_{Freq} tf(w)$$

and similarly for $Rarity$.

In both cases, the aesthetic's value is computed via an equation similar to the following:

$$a(w) = \omega_{Freq}(w)\omega_{Rarity}(w)\gamma_{Range} b$$

where $a(w)$ is either font size or opacity, and b is some base value of the aesthetic (scaled by a dynamic range slider, γ_{Range}) and the weights for frequency and rarity of the word. In this manner, the weights are multiplicative, so interactions between the variables (e.g., tf*idf) are apparent.

Though unigram statistics are informative, seeing the unigrams in context is also important for many inference tasks. To enable this, we use reservoir sampling (Vitter, 1985) to maintain a representative sample of the observed occurrences of each word in context, which the user can view by clicking on the word in the wordcloud display.

Examples of the dynamic wordcloud in various settings can be found in Figure 1, using a set of tweets containing "Orioles". The left wordcloud has tf mapped to size, the center with idf mapped to size, and the right with both high tf and high idf mapped to size. We only manipulate the size aesthetic, since the opacity aesthetic is sometimes hard to interpret in print. To fit the wordclouds to the small format, various values for τ_{Freq} and τ_{Rarity} are employed, and order is varied – the left is ordered in descending order in terms of frequency, the center is ordered in descending order in terms of rarity, and the right is in alphabetical order.

8 Vennclouds

Question **(2)** – "how are these corpora related" requires only a single change to the dynamic single wordcloud described in §7. We refer to two corpora, *left* and *right*, which we abbreviate L and R (perhaps a set of tweets containing "Orioles" for *left* and those containing "Nationals" for *right* as in Figure 2). For the *right* documents, let $R = \{d_1, ..., d_{n_R}\}$ so $|R| = n_R$ and let T_R be the total number of tokens in all the documents in R

$$T_R = \sum_{d \in R} |T_d|$$

We separate the wordcloud display into three regions, one devoted to words most closely associated with R, one devoted to words most closely associated with L, and one for words that should be associated with both. "Association" here can be defined in a number of ways, but for the nonce we define it as the probability of occurrence in that corpus – essentially term frequency, normalized by corpus length. Normalizing by length is required to prevent bias incurred when the corpora are different sizes ($T_L \neq T_R$). Specifically, we define the number of times w occurs in *left* (tf) as

$$tf_L(w) = \sum_{d_i \in L} T(w, d_i)$$

and this quantity normalized by the number of tokens in L,

$$\overline{tf_L}(w) = tf_L(w)/T_L$$

and this quantity as it relates to the term frequency of this w in both corpora

$$\overline{tf_{L|R}}(w) = \frac{tf_L(w)}{tf_L(w) + tf_R(w)}$$

Each word is only displayed once in the Venncloud (see Figure 2, so if a word (w) only occurs in R, it is always present in the *right* region, and likewise for L and *left*. If w is in both L and R, we examine the proportion of documents in each that w is in and use this to determine in which region it should be displayed. In order to deal with

Figure 2: Three example Vennclouds, with tweets containing "Orioles" on the left, "Nationals" on the right, and common words in the middle. From top to bottom we allow progressively larger common clouds. The large common words make sense – both teams played a **Chicago** team and made the **playoffs** in the time covered by these corpora.

the cases where w occurs in approximately similar proportions of *left* and *right* documents, we have a *center* region (in the center in Figure 2). We define a threshold (τ_{Common}) to concretely define "approximately similar". Specifically,

- if $tf_R(w) = 0$, w is displayed in *left*.
- if $tf_L(w) = 0$, w is displayed in *right*.
- if $tf_R(w) > 0$ and $tf_L(w) > 0$,
  - if $\overline{tf_{R|L}}(w) > \overline{tf_{L|R}}(w) + \tau_{Common}$, w is displayed in *right*.
  - if $\overline{tf_{L|R}}(w) > \overline{tf_{R|L}}(w) + \tau_{Common}$, w is displayed in *left*.
  - Otherwise, w is displayed in *center*.

The user is given a slider to control τ_{Common}, allowing them to determine what value of "approximately similar" best fits the data and their task at hand.

9 Anecdotal Evaluation

We have not yet done a proper psychophysical evaluation of the utility of dynamic wordclouds

Figure 3: Screenshot of a Venncloud, with controls. The sliders are accessible from the buttons across the top, displaying as a floating window above the wordcloud itself (replacing the current display of the legend). Also note the examples in the lower left and right corners, accessed by clicking on a word of interest (in this case "Sox").

and Vennclouds for various tasks as compared to their static counterparts (and other visualizations). In part, this is because such an evaluation requires selection of inference tasks to be examined, precisely what we do not claim to be able to do. We leave for future work the creation and evaluation of a representative sample of such inference tasks.

We strongly believe that the plural of anecdote is not data – so these anecdotes are intended as illustrations of use, rather than some data regarding utility. The dynamic wordclouds and Vennclouds were used on data from across the spectrum, from tweets to Shakespeare and political speeches to health-related conversations in developing nations. In Shakespeare, character and place names can easily be highlighted with one set of slider settings (high $tf*idf$), while comparisons of stopwords are made apparent with another (high tf, no idf). Emerging from the debates between Mitt Romney and Barack Obama are the common themes that they discuss using similar (economics) and dissimilar language (Obama talks about the "affordable care act" and Romney calls it "Obamacare"). These wordclouds were also used to do some introspection on the output of classifiers in sentiment analysis (Mitchell et al., 2013) and mental health research (Coppersmith et al., 2014b) to expose the linguistic signals that give rise to successful (and unsuccessful) classification.

10 Conclusions and Future Directions

Exploratory data analysis tools for human language data and inference tasks have long lagged behind their numerical counterparts, and here we investigate another step towards filling that need. Rather than determining the optimal wordcloud, we enable the wordcloud viewer to adapt the visualization to the data and inference task at hand. We suspect that the pendulum of control has swung too far, and that there is a subset of the possible control configurations that produce *useful* and *informative* wordclouds. Work is underway to collect feedback via instrumented dynamic wordclouds and Vennclouds as they are used for various inference tasks to address this.

Previous research, logic, and intuition were used to create this step, though it requires further improvement and validation. We provide anecdotes about the usefulness of these dynamic wordclouds, but those anecdotes do not provide sufficient evidence that this method is somehow more efficient (in terms of human time) than existing methods. To make such claims, a controlled human-factors study is required, investigating (for a particular inference task) how this method affects the job of an exploratory data analyst. In the meantime, we hope making the code freely available[1] will better enable our fellow researchers to perform principled exploratory data analysis of human language content quickly and encourage a deeper understanding of data, within and across disciplines.

Acknowledgments

We would like to thank Carey Priebe for insightful discussions on exploratory data analysis,

[1] from https://github.com/Coppersmith/vennclouds

Aleksander Yelskiy, Jacqueline Aguilar, Kristy Hollingshead for their analysis, comments, and improvements on early versions, and Ainsley R. Coppersmith for permitting this research to progress in her early months.

References

Scott Bateman, Carl Gutwin, and Miguel Nacenta. 2008. Seeing things in the clouds: the effect of visual features on tag cloud selections. In *Proceedings of the nineteenth ACM conference on Hypertext and hypermedia*, pages 193–202. ACM.

Quim Castella and Charles A. Sutton. 2013. Word storms: Multiples of word clouds for visual comparison of documents. *CoRR*, abs/1301.0503.

Cindy Chung and James W Pennebaker. 2007. The psychological functions of function words. *Social communication*, pages 343–359.

Christopher Collins, Fernanda B Viegas, and Martin Wattenberg. 2009. Parallel tag clouds to explore and analyze faceted text corpora. In *Visual Analytics Science and Technology, 2009. VAST 2009. IEEE Symposium on*, pages 91–98. IEEE.

Glen Coppersmith, Mark Dredze, and Craig Harman. 2014a. Quantifying mental health signals in twitter. In *Proceedings of ACL Workshop on Computational Linguistics and Clinical Psychology*. Association for Computational Linguistics.

Glen Coppersmith, Craig Harman, and Mark Dredze. 2014b. Measuring post traumatic stress disorder in Twitter. In *Proceedings of the International AAAI Conference on Weblogs and Social Media (ICWSM)*.

Weiwei Cui, Yingcai Wu, Shixia Liu, Furu Wei, Michelle X Zhou, and Huamin Qu. 2010. Context preserving dynamic word cloud visualization. In *Pacific Visualization Symposium (PacificVis), 2010 IEEE*, pages 121–128. IEEE.

Jason Davies. 2013. Wordcloud generator using d3, April.

Micah Dubinko, Ravi Kumar, Joseph Magnani, Jasmine Novak, Prabhakar Raghavan, and Andrew Tomkins. 2007. Visualizing tags over time. *ACM Transactions on the Web (TWEB)*, 1(2):7.

Jason Feinberg. 2013. Wordle, April.

Patrick Juola. 2006. Authorship attribution. *Foundations and Trends in information Retrieval*, 1(3):233–334.

Kathrin Knautz, Simone Soubusta, and Wolfgang G Stock. 2010. Tag clusters as information retrieval interfaces. In *System Sciences (HICSS), 2010 43rd Hawaii International Conference on*, pages 1–10. IEEE.

Bongshin Lee, Nathalie Henry Riche, Amy K Karlson, and Sheelagh Carpendale. 2010. Sparkclouds: Visualizing trends in tag clouds. *Visualization and Computer Graphics, IEEE Transactions on*, 16(6):1182–1189.

Margaret Mitchell, Jacqueline Aguilar, Theresa Wilson, and Benjamin Van Durme. 2013. Open domain targeted sentiment. In *Proceedings of the 2013 Conference on Empirical Methods in Natural Language Processing*, pages 1643–1654. Association for Computational Linguistics.

Saša Petrovic, Miles Osborne, Richard McCreadie, Craig Macdonald, Iadh Ounis, and Luke Shrimpton. 2013. Can twitter replace newswire for breaking news. In *Seventh International AAAI Conference on Weblogs and Social Media*.

Paul Rayson and Roger Garside. 2000. Comparing corpora using frequency profiling. In *Proceedings of the workshop on Comparing Corpora*, pages 1–6. Association for Computational Linguistics.

AW Rivadeneira, Daniel M Gruen, Michael J Muller, and David R Millen. 2007. Getting our head in the clouds: toward evaluation studies of tagclouds. In *Proceedings of the SIGCHI conference on Human factors in computing systems*, pages 995–998. ACM.

Johann Schrammel, Michael Leitner, and Manfred Tscheligi. 2009. Semantically structured tag clouds: an empirical evaluation of clustered presentation approaches. In *Proceedings of the 27th international conference on Human factors in computing systems*, pages 2037–2040. ACM.

Christin Seifert, Barbara Kump, Wolfgang Kienreich, Gisela Granitzer, and Michael Granitzer. 2008. On the beauty and usability of tag clouds. In *Information Visualisation, 2008. IV'08. 12th International Conference*, pages 17–25. IEEE.

James Sinclair and Michael Cardew-Hall. 2008. The folksonomy tag cloud: when is it useful? *Journal of Information Science*, 34(1):15–29.

Aidan Slingsby, Jason Dykes, Jo Wood, and Keith Clarke. 2007. Interactive tag maps and tag clouds for the multiscale exploration of large spatio-temporal datasets. In *Information Visualization, 2007. IV'07. 11th International Conference*, pages 497–504. IEEE.

Fernanda B Viégas and Martin Wattenberg. 2008. Timelines tag clouds and the case for vernacular visualization. *interactions*, 15(4):49–52.

Jeffrey S Vitter. 1985. Random sampling with a reservoir. *ACM Transactions on Mathematical Software (TOMS)*, 11(1):37–57.

Hadley Wickham. 2009. *ggplot2: elegant graphics for data analysis*. Springer Publishing Company, Incorporated.

Active Learning with Constrained Topic Model

Yi Yang
Northwestern University
yiyang@u.northwestern.edu

Shimei Pan
IBM T. J. Watson Research Center
shimei@us.ibm.com

Doug Downey
Northwestern University
ddowney@eecs.northwestern.edu

Kunpeng Zhang
University of Illinois at Chicago
kzhang6@uic.edu

Abstract

Latent Dirichlet Allocation (LDA) is a topic modeling tool that automatically discovers topics from a large collection of documents. It is one of the most popular text analysis tools currently in use. In practice however, the topics discovered by LDA do not always make sense to end users. In this extended abstract, we propose an active learning framework that interactively and iteratively acquires user feedback to improve the quality of learned topics. We conduct experiments to demonstrate its effectiveness with simulated user input on a benchmark dataset.

1 Introduction

Statistical topic models such as Latent Dirichlet Allocation (LDA) (Blei et al., 2003) provide powerful tools for uncovering hidden thematic patterns in text and are useful for representing and summarizing the contents of large document collections. However, when using topic models in practice, users often face one critical problem: topics discovered by the model do not always make sense. A topic may contain thematically unrelated words. Moreover, two thematic related words may appear in different topics. This is mainly because the objective function optimized by LDA may not reflect human judgments of topic quality (Boyd-Graber et al., 2009).

Potentially, we can solve these problems by incorporating additional user guidance or domain knowledge in topic modeling. With standard LDA however, it is impossible for users to interact with the model and provide feedback. (Hu et al., 2011) proposed an interactive topic modeling framework that allows users to add word must-links. However, it has several limitations. Since the vocabulary size of a large document collection can be very large, users may need to annotate a large number of word constraints for this method to be effective. Thus, this process can be very tedious. More importantly, it cannot handle polysemes. For example, the word "pound" can refer to either a currency or a unit of mass. If a user adds a must-link between "pound" and another financial term, then he/she cannot add a must-link between "pound" and any measurement terms. Since word must-links are added without context, there is no way to disambiguate them. As a result, word constraints frequently are not as effective as document constraints.

Active learning (Settles, 2010) provides a useful framework which allows users to iteratively give feedback to the model to improve its quality. In general, with the same amount of human labeling, active learning often results in a better model than that learned by an off-line method.

In this extended abstract, we propose an active learning framework for LDA. It is based on a new constrained topic modeling framework which is capable of handling pairwise document constraints. We present several design choices and the pros and cons of each choice. We also conduct simulated experiments to demonstrate the effectiveness of the approach.

2 Active Learning With Constrained Topic Modeling

In this section, we first summarize our work on constrained topic modeling. Then, we introduce an active topic learning framework that employs constrained topic modeling.

In LDA, a document's topic distribution $\vec{\theta}$ is drawn from a Dirichlet distribution with prior $\vec{\alpha}$. A simple and commonly used Dirichlet distribution uses a symmetric $\vec{\alpha}$ prior. However, (Wallach et al., 2009) has shown that an asymmetric Dirichlet prior over the document-topic distributions $\vec{\theta}$ and a symmetric Dirichlet prior over the topic-word distributions $\vec{\phi}$ yield significant improvements in model performance. Our constrained topic model uses asymmetric priors to encode constraints.

To incorporate user feedback, we focus on two

Proceedings of the Workshop on Interactive Language Learning, Visualization, and Interfaces, pages 30–33,
Baltimore, Maryland, USA, June 27, 2014. ©2014 Association for Computational Linguistics

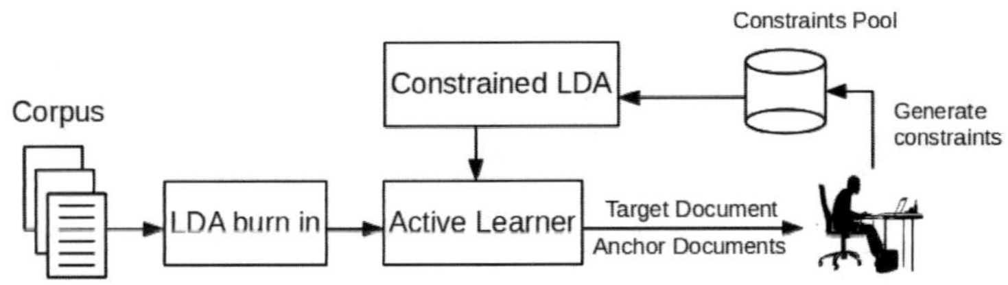

Figure 1: Diagram illustrating the topic model active learning framework.

types of document constraints. A **must-link** between two documents indicates that they belong to the same topics, while a **cannot-link** indicates that they belong to different topics.

Previously, we proposed a constrained LDA framework called cLDA,[1] which is capable of incorporating pairwise document constraints. Given pairwise document constraints, the topic distribution of a document cannot be assumed to be independently sampled. More specifically, we denote the collection of documents as $\mathcal{D} = \{d_1, d_2, ..., d_N\}$. We also denote $\mathcal{M}_i \in \mathcal{D}$ as the set of documents sharing must-links with document d_i, and $\mathcal{C}_i \in \mathcal{D}$ as the set of documents sharing cannot-links with document d_i. $\vec{\theta_i}$ is the topic distribution of d_i, and $\vec{\alpha}$ is the global document-topic hyper-parameter shared by all documents.

Given the documents in $\mathcal{M}_i$, we introduce an auxiliary variable $\vec{\alpha_i}^{\mathcal{M}}$:

$$\vec{\alpha_i}^{\mathcal{M}} = T * \frac{1}{|\mathcal{M}_i|} \sum_{j \in \mathcal{M}_i} \vec{\theta_j}, \quad (1)$$

where T controls the concentration parameters. The larger the value of T is, the closer $\vec{\theta_i}$ is to the average of $\vec{\theta_j}$'s.

Given the documents in $\mathcal{C}_i$, we introduce another auxiliary variable:

$$\vec{\alpha_i}^{\mathcal{C}} = T * \arg_{\vec{\theta_i}} \max \min_{j \in \mathcal{C}_i} KL(\vec{\theta_i}, \vec{\theta_j}), \quad (2)$$

where $KL(\vec{\theta_i}, \vec{\theta_j})$ is the KL-divergence between two distributions $\vec{\theta_i}$ and $\vec{\theta_j}$. This means we choose a vector that is maximally far away from $\mathcal{C}_i$, in terms of KL divergence to its nearest neighbor in $\mathcal{C}_i$.

In such a way, we force documents sharing must-links to have similar topic distributions while documents sharing cannot-links to have dissimilar topic distributions. Note that it also encodes constraint as soft preference rather than hard constraint. We use Collapsed Gibbs Sampling for LDA inference. During Gibbs Sampling, instead of always drawing $\vec{\theta_i}$ from $Dirichlet(\vec{\alpha})$, we draw $\vec{\theta_i}$ based on the following distribution:

$$\vec{\theta_i} \sim Dir(\eta\vec{\alpha} + \eta_{\mathcal{M}}\vec{\alpha_i}^{\mathcal{M}} + \eta_{\mathcal{C}}\vec{\alpha_i}^{\mathcal{C}}) = Dir(\vec{\alpha_i}). \quad (3)$$

Here, η_g, $\eta_{\mathcal{M}}$ and $\eta_{\mathcal{C}}$ are the weights to control the trade-off among the three terms. In our experiment, we choose $T = 100$, $\eta_g = \eta_{\mathcal{M}} = \eta_{\mathcal{C}} = 1$.

Our evaluation has shown that cLDA is effective in improving topic model quality. For example, it achieved a significant topic classification error reduction on the 20 Newsgroup dataset. Also, topics learned by cLDA are more coherent than those learned by standard LDA.

2.1 Active Learning with User Interaction

In this subsection, we present an active learning framework to iteratively acquire constraints from users. As shown in Figure 1, given a document collection, the framework first runs standard LDA with a burnin component. Since it uses a Gibbs sampler (Griffiths and Steyvers, 2004) to infer topic samples for each word token, it usually takes hundreds of iterations for the sampler to converge to a stable state. Based on the results of the burnt-in model, the system generates a target document and a set of anchor documents for a user to annotate. Target document is a document on which the active learner solicits user feedback, and anchor documents are representatives of a topic model's latent topics. If a large portion of the word tokens in a document belongs to topic i, we say the document is an *anchor* document for topic i.

A user judges the content of the target and the anchor documents and then informs the system whether the target document is similar to any of the anchor documents. The user interface is designed so that the user can drag the target document near an anchor document if she considers both to be the same topic. Currently, one target document can be must-linked to only one anchor document. Since it is possbile to have multiple topics in one document, in the future, we will allow user to add must links between one target and mulitple anchor documents. After adding one or more must-links, the

[1] currently in submission.

system automatically adds cannot-links between the target document and the rest anchor documents.

Given this input, the system adds them to a constraint pool. It then uses cLDA to incorporate these constraints and generates an updated topic model. Based on the new topic model, the system chooses a new target document and several new anchor documents for the user to annotate. This process continues until the user is satisfied with the resulting topic model.

How to choose the target and anchor documents are the key questions that we consider in the next subsections.

2.2 Target Document Selection

A target document is defined as a document on which the active learner solicits user feedback. We have investigated several strategies for selecting a target document.

Random: The active learner randomly selects a document from the corpus. Although this strategy is the simplest, it may not be efficient since the model may have enough information about the document already.

MaxEntropy: The entropy of a document d is computed as $H_d = -\sum_{i=1}^{K} \theta_{dk} \log \theta_{dk}$, where K is the number of topics, and θ is model's document-topic distribution. Therefore, the system will select a document about which it is most confused. A uniform θ implies that the model has no topic information about the document and thus assigns equal probability to all topics.

MinLikelihood: The likelihood of a document d is computed as $L_d = (\sum_{i=1}^{N} \sum_{k=1}^{K} \phi_{ki}\theta_{dk})/N$, where N is the number of tokens in d, and ϕ is model's topic-word distribution. Since the overall likelihood of the input documents is the objective function LDA aims to maximize, using this criteria, the system will choose a document that is most difficult for which the current model achieves the lowest objective score.

2.3 Anchor Documents Selection

Given a target document d, the active learner then generates one or more anchor documents based on the target document's topic distribution θ_d. It filters out topics with trivial value in θ_d and extracts an anchor topic set T_{anc} which only contains topics with non-trivial value in θ_d. A trivial θ_{di} means that the mass of ith component in θ_d is neglectable, which indicates that the model rarely assign topic i to document d. For each topic t in T_{anc}, the active learner selects an anchor document who has minimum Euclidean distance with an ideal anchor θ'_t. In the ideal anchor θ'_t, all the components are zero except the value of the t_{th} component is 1. For example, if a target document d's θ_d is $\{0.5, 0.3, 0.03, 0.02, 0.15\}$ in a $K = 5$ topic model, the active learner would generate $T_{anc} = \{0, 1, 4\}$ and for each t in T_{anc}, an anchor document.

However, it is possible that some topics learned by LDA are only "background" topics which have significant non-trivial probabilities over many documents (Song et al., 2009). Since background topics are often uninteresting ones, we use a weighted anchor topic selection method to filter them. A weighted k_{th} component of θ'_{dk} for document d is defined as follows: $\theta'_{dk} = \theta_{dk} / \sum_{i=0}^{D} \theta_{ik}$. Therefore, instead of keeping the topics with non-trivial values, we keep those whose weighted values are non-trivial.

3 Evaluation

In this section, we evaluate our active learning framework. Topic models are often evaluated using perplexity on held-out test data. However, recent work (Boyd-Graber et al., 2009; Chuang et al., 2013) has shown that human judgment sometimes is contrary to the perplexity measure. Following (Mimno et al., 2011), we employ Topic Coherence, a metric which was shown to be highly consistent with human judgment, to measure a topic model's quality. It relies upon word co-occurrence statistics within documents, and does not depend on external resources or human labeling.

We followed (Basu et al., 2004) to create a `Mix3` sub-dataset from the 20 Newsgroups data[2], which consists of two newsgroups with similar topics (rec.sport.hockey, rec.sport.baseball) and one with a distinctive topic (sci.space). We use this dataset to evaluate the effectiveness of the proposed framework.

3.1 Simulated Experiments

We first burn-in LDA for 500 iterations. Then for each additional iteration, the active learner generates one query which consists of one target document and one or more anchor documents. We simulate user feedback using the documents' ground truth labels. If a target document has the same label as one of the anchor documents, we add a must-link between them. We also add cannot-links between the target document and the rest of the anchor documents. All these constraints are added into a constraint pool. We also augment the constraint pool with derived constraints. For example, due to transitivity, if there is a must-link between (a, b) and (b, c), then we add

[2]Available at `http://people.csail.mit.edu/jrennie/20Newsgroups`

Topic	Words
1	writes, like, think, good, know, better, even, people, run, hit
2	space, nasa, system, gov, launch, orbit, moon, earth, access, data
3	game, play, hockey, season, league, fun, wing, cup, shot, score
1	baseball, hit, won, shot, hitter, base, pitching, cub, ball, yankee
2	space, nasa, system, gov, launch, obit, moon, earth, mission, shuttle
3	hockey, nhl, playoff, star, wing, cup, king, detroit, ranger

Table 1: Ten most probable words of each topic before (above) and after active learning (below).

a must link between (a, c). We simulate the process for 100 iterations to acquire constraints. After that, we keep cLDA running for 400 more iterations with the acquired constraints until it converges.

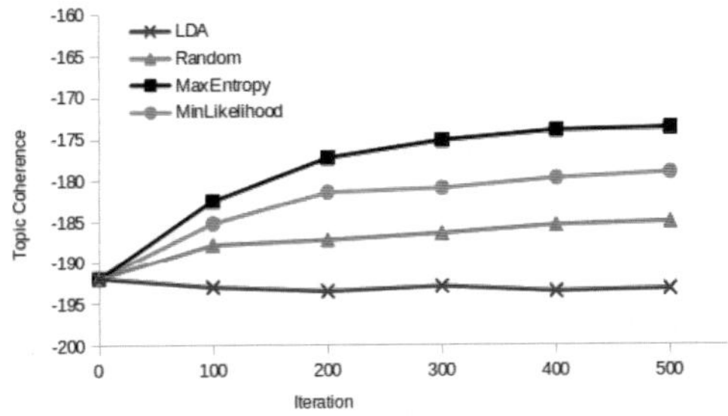

Figure 2: Topic coherence with different number of iterations.

Figure 2 shows the topic coherence scores for different target document selection strategies. This result indicates 1). MaxEntropy has the best topic coherence score. 2). All active learning strategies outperform standard LDA, and the results are statistically significant at $p = 0.05$. With standard LDA, 500 more iterations without any constraints does not improve the topic coherence. However, by active learning with cLDA for 500 iterations, the topic coherences are significantly improved.

Using MaxEntropy target document selection method, we demonstrate the improvement of the most probable topic keywords before and after active learning. Table 1 shows that before active learning, topic 1's most probable words are incoherent and thus it is difficult to determine the meaning of the topic . After active learning, in contrast, topic 1's most probable words become more consistent with a "baseball" topic. This example suggests that the active learning framework that interactively and iteratively acquires pairwise document constraints is effective in improving the topic model's quality.

4 Conclusion

We presented a novel active learning framework for LDA that employs constrained topic modeling to actively incorporate user feedback encoded as pairwise document constraints. With simulated user input, our preliminary results demonstrate the effectiveness of the framework on a benchmark dataset. In the future, we will perform a formal user study in which real users will interact with the system to iteratively refine topic models.

Acknowledgments

This work was supported in part by DARPA contract D11AP00268.

References

Sugato Basu, A. Banjeree, ER. Mooney, Arindam Banerjee, and Raymond J. Mooney. 2004. Active semi-supervision for pairwise constrained clustering. In *SDM*, pages 333–344.

David M. Blei, Andrew Y. Ng, and Michael I. Jordan. 2003. Latent dirichlet allocation. *Journal of Machine Learning Research*, 3:993–1022.

Jordan Boyd-Graber, Jonathan Chang, Sean Gerrish, Chong Wang, and David Blei. 2009. Reading tea leaves: How humans interpret topic models. In *NIPS*.

Jason Chuang, Sonal Gupta, Christopher D. Manning, and Jeffrey Heer. 2013. Topic model diagnostics: Assessing domain relevance via topical alignment. In *ICML*.

T. L. Griffiths and M. Steyvers. 2004. Finding scientific topics. *Proceedings of the National Academy of Sciences*, 101(Suppl. 1):5228–5235.

Yuening Hu, Jordan Boyd-Graber, and Brianna Satinoff. 2011. Interactive topic modeling. In *ACL*, pages 248–257.

David Mimno, Hanna M. Wallach, Edmund Talley, Miriam Leenders, and Andrew McCallum. 2011. Optimizing semantic coherence in topic models. In *EMNLP*, pages 262–272.

Burr Settles. 2010. Active learning literature survey. Technical report, University of Wisconsin Madison.

Yangqiu Song, Shimei Pan, Shixia Liu, Michelle X. Zhou, and Weihong Qian. 2009. Topic and keyword re-ranking for lda-based topic modeling. In *CIKM*, pages 1757–1760.

Hanna M. Wallach, David M. Mimno, and Andrew McCallum. 2009. Rethinking lda: Why priors matter. In *NIPS*, pages 1973–1981.

GLANCE Visualizes Lexical Phenomena for Language Learning

Mei-Hua Chen[*], **Shih-Ting Huang**[+], **Ting-Hui Kao**[+], **Sun-Wen Chiu**[+], **Tzu-His Yen**[+]
[*] Department of Foreign Languages and Literature, Hua Fan University, Taipei, Taiwan, R.O.C. 22301
[+] Department of Computer Science, National Tsing Hua University, HsinChu, Taiwan, R.O.C. 30013
{chen.meihua,koromiko1104,maxis1718,chiuhsunwen, joseph.yen}@gmail.com

Abstract

Facilitating vocabulary knowledge is a challenging aspect for language learners. Although current corpus-based reference tools provide authentic contextual clues, the plain text format is not conducive to fully illustrating some lexical phenomena. Thus, this paper proposes GLANCE [1], a text visualization tool, to present a large amount of lexical phenomena using charts and graphs, aimed at helping language learners understand a word quickly and intuitively. To evaluate the effectiveness of the system, we designed interfaces to allow comparison between text and graphics presentation, and conducted a preliminary user study with ESL students. The results show that the visualized display is of greater benefit to the understanding of word characteristics than textual display.

1 Introduction

Vocabulary is a challenging aspect for language learners to master. Extended word knowledge, such as word polarity and position, is not widely available in traditional dictionaries. Thus, for most language learners, it is very difficult to have a good command of such lexical phenomena.

Current linguistics software programs use large corpus data to advance language learning. The use of corpora exposes learners to authentic contextual clues and lets them discover patterns or collocations of words from contextual clues (Partington, 1998). However, a huge amount of data can be overwhelming and time-consuming (Yeh et al., 2007) for language learners to induce rules or patterns. On the other hand, some lexical phenomena seem unable to be comprehended fast and directly in plain text format (Koo, 2006). For example, in the British National Corpus (2007), "however" seems more negative than "but". Also, compared with "but", "however" appears more frequently at the beginning of a sentence.

With this in mind, we proposed GLANCE[1], a text visualization tool, which presents corpus data using charts and graphs to help language learners understand the lexical phenomena of a word quickly and intuitively. In this paper, we focused on five types of lexical phenomena: polarity, position, POS, form and discipline, which will be detailed in the Section 3. Given a single query word, the GLANCE system shows graphical representations of its lexical phenomena sequentially within a single web page.

Additionally we believe that the use of graphics also facilitates the understanding of the differences between two words. Taking this into consideration, we introduce a comparison mode to help learners differentiate two words at a glance. Allowing two word input, GLANCE draws the individual representative graphs for both words and presents these graphs in a two-column view. The display of parallel graphs depicts the distinctions between the two words clearly.

2 Related Work

Corpus-based language learning has widened the perspectives in second and foreign language education, such as vocabulary learning (Wood, 2001). In past decades, various corpus-based reference tools have been developed. For example, WordSmith (Scott, 2000), Compleat Lexical Tutor (Cobb, 2007), GRASP (Huang et al., 2011), PREFER (Chen et al, 2012).

Recently, some interactive visualization tools have been developed for the purpose of illustrating various linguistic phenomena. Three exam-

[1] http://glance-it.herokuapp.com/

Proceedings of the Workshop on Interactive Language Learning, Visualization, and Interfaces, pages 34–37,
Baltimore, Maryland, USA, June 27, 2014. ©2014 Association for Computational Linguistics

ples are Word Tree, a visual concordance (Wattenberg and Viégas, 2008), WORDGRAPH, a visual tool for context-sensitive word choice (Riehmann et al., 2012) and Visual Thesaurus, a 3D interactive reference tool (ThinkMap Inc., 2005).

3 Design of the GLANCE System

The GLANCE system consists of several components of corpus data visualization. We design and implement these visualization modules separately to ensure all graphs are simple and clear enough for users to capture and understand the lexical phenomena quickly.

In this paper, we use the d3.js (Data-Driven Documents) (Bostock et al., 2011) to visualize the data. The d3.js enables direct inspection and manipulation of a standard document object model (DOM) so that we are able to transform numeric data into various types of graphs when fitting these data to other visualization tools. In this section, we describe the ways we extract the data from the corpus and how we translate these data into informative graphs.

3.1 Data Preprocessing

We use the well-formed corpus, the BNC, to extract the data. In order to obtain the Part-of-speech tags for each text, we use the GENIA tagger (Tsuruoka et al., 2005) to analyze the sentences of the BNC and build a list of *<POS-tag, frequency>* pairs for each word in the BNC. Also the BNC contains the classification code assigned to the text in a genre-based analysis carried out at Lancaster University by Lee (2001). For each word, the classification codes are aggregated to a list of *<code, frequency>* pairs.

3.2 Visualization of Lexical Phenomena

Polarity

A word may carry different sentiment polarities (i.e., positive, negative and objective). To help users quickly determine the proper sentiment polarity of a word, we introduce the sentiment polarity information of SentiWordNet (Baccianella et al., 2010) into our system. For each synset of a word, GLANCE displays the polarity in a bar with three different colors. The individual length of the three parts in the bar corresponds to the polarity scores of a synset (Figure 1).

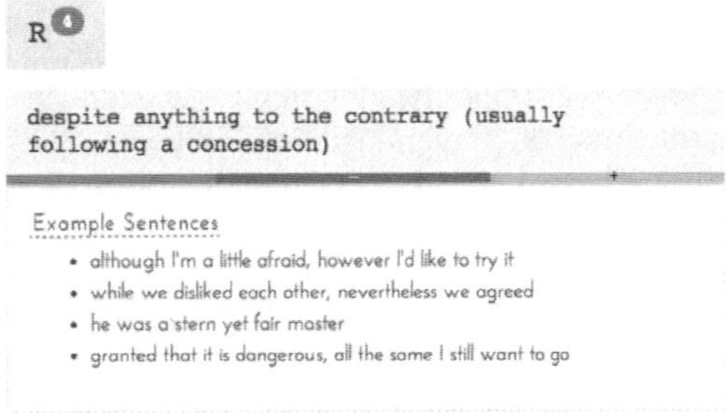

Figure 1. Representation of sentiment polarity

Position

The word position in a sentence is also an important lexical phenomenon. By calculating the word position in each sentence, we then obtain the location distribution. GLANCE visualizes the distribution information of a word using a bar chart. Figure 2 shows a plot of distribution of word position on the x-axis against the word frequency on the y-axis.

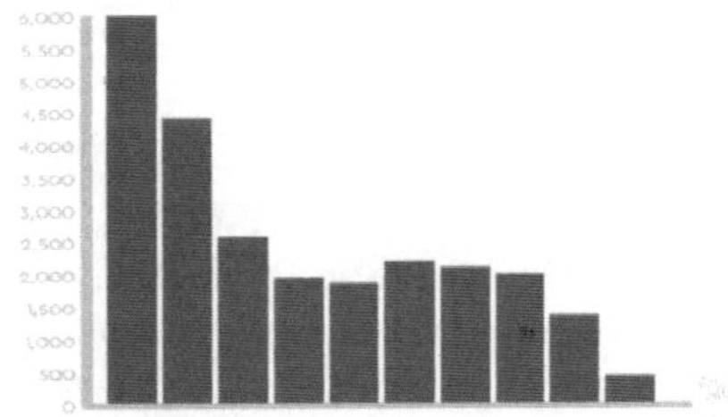

Figure 2. Distribution of word position

Part Of Speech (POS)

A lexical item may have more than one part of speech. Knowing the distribution of POS helps users quickly understand the general usage of a word.

GLANCE displays a pie chart for each word to differentiate between its parts of speech. We use the maximum likelihood probability of a POS tag for a word as the arc length of the pie chart (Figure 3).

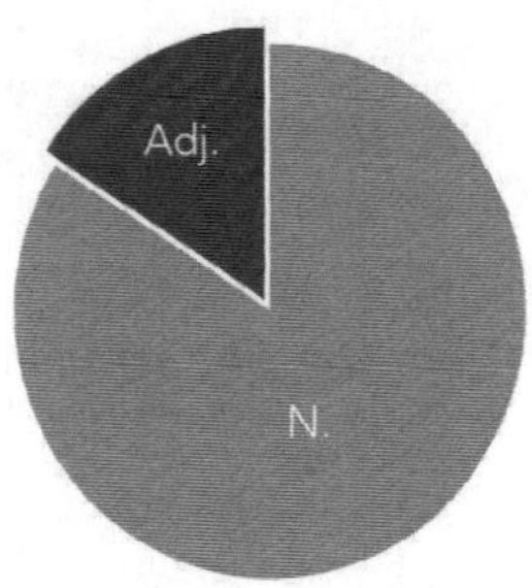

Figure 3. POS representation

Form

The levels of formality of written and spoken language are different, which also confuse language learners. Pie charts are used to illustrate the proportion of written and spoken English of individual words as shown in Figure 4.

We derive the frequencies of both forms from the BNC classification code for each word. The arc length of each sector is proportional to the maximum likelihood probability of forms.

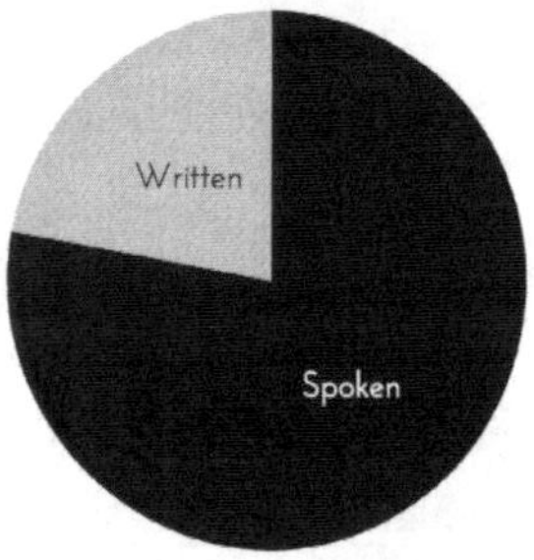

Figure 4. Form representation

Discipline

Similar to language form, the discipline information (e.g., newspaper or fiction) was gathered from the BNC classification code. The relations of the disciplines of a word are presented using a sunburst graph, a radial space-filling tree layout implemented with prefuse (Heer et al., 2005). In the sunburst graph (Figure 5.), each level corresponds to the relation of the disciplines of a certain word. The farther the level is away from the center, the more specific the discipline is. Each level is given equal width, but the circular angle swept out by a discipline corresponds to the frequency of the disciplines.

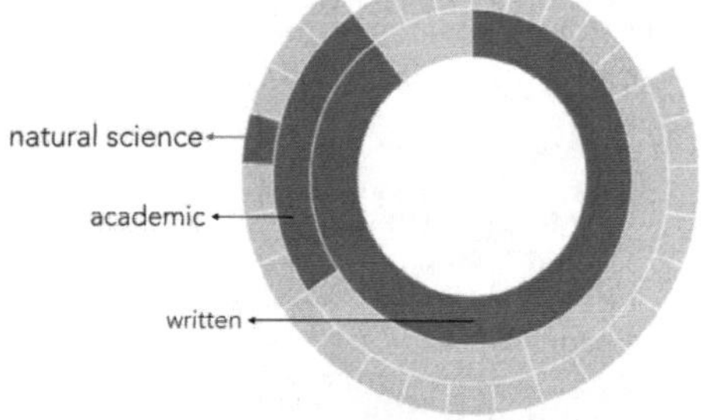

Figure 5. Discipline relations

4 Results

4.1 Experimental Setting

We performed a preliminary user study to assess the efficiency of our system in assisting language learners in grasping lexical phenomena. To examine the effectiveness of visualization, we built a textual interface for comparison with the graphical interface.

Ten pre-intermediate ESL college students participated in the study. A total of six pairs of similar words were listed on the worksheet. After being introduced to GLANCE, all students were randomly divided into two groups. One group was required to consult the first three pairs using the graphical interface and the second three pairs the textual interface, and vice versa. The participants were allowed a maximum of one minute per pair, which meets the goal of this study of quickly glancing at the graphics and grasping the concepts of words. Then a test sheet containing the same six similar word pairs was used to examine the extent of students' word understanding. Note that during the test, no tool supports were provided. The student scored one point if he gave the correct answers to each question. In other words he would be awarded 6 points (the highest number of points) if he provided all the correct answers. They also completed a questionnaire, described below, evaluating the system.

4.2 Experimental Results

To determine the effectiveness of visualization of lexical phenomena, the students' average scores were used as performance indicators. Students achieved the average score 61.9 and 45.0 out of 100.00 after consulting the graphic interface and textual interface respectively. Overall, the visualized display of word characteristics outperformed the textual version.

The questionnaire revealed that all the participants showed a positive attitude to visualized word information. Further analyses showed that all ten participants appreciated the position display and nine of them the polarity and form displays. In short, the graphical display of lexical phenomena in GLANCE results in faster assimilation and understanding of word information. Moreover, the participants suggested several interesting aspects for improving the GLANCE system. For example, they preferred bilingual environment, further information concerning antonyms, more example sentences, and increased detail in the sunburst representation of disciplines.

5 Conclusion and Future Work

In this paper, we proposed GLANCE, a text visualization tool, which provides graphical display of corpus data. Our goal is to assist language learners in glancing at the graphics and grasping the lexical knowledge quickly and intuitively. To evaluate the efficiency and effectiveness of GLANCE, we conducted a preliminary user study with ten non-native ESL learners. The results revealed that visualization format outperformed plain text format.

Many avenues exist for future research and improvement. We attempt to expand the single word to phrase level. For example, the collocation behaviors are expected to be deduced and displayed. Moreover, we are interested in supporting more lexical phenomena, such as hyponyms, to provide learners with more lexical relations of the word with other words.

Reference

Baccianella, S., Esuli, A., & Sebastiani, F. (2010, May). SentiWordNet 3.0: An Enhanced Lexical Resource for Sentiment Analysis and Opinion Mining. In *LREC* (Vol. 10, pp. 2200-2204).

Bostock, M., Ogievetsky, V., & Heer, J. (2011). D^3 data-driven documents. *Visualization and Computer Graphics, IEEE Transactions on*, *17*(12), 2301-2309.

Chen, M. H., Huang, S. T., Huang, C. C., Liou, H. C., & Chang, J. S. (2012, June). PREFER: using a graph-based approach to generate paraphrases for language learning. In *Proceedings of the Seventh Workshop on Building Educational Applications Using NLP* (pp. 80-85). Association for Computational Linguistics.

Cobb, T. (2007). The compleat lexical tutor. *Retrieved September*, *22*, 2009.

Heer, J., Card, S. K., & Landay, J. A. (2005, April). Prefuse: a toolkit for interactive information visualization. In *Proceedings of the SIGCHI conference on Human factors in computing systems* (pp. 421-430). ACM.

Huang, C. C., Chen, M. H., Huang, S. T., Liou, H. C., & Chang, J. S. (2011, June). GRASP: grammar- and syntax-based pattern-finder in CALL. In *Proceedings of the 6th Workshop on Innovative Use of NLP for Building Educational Applications* (pp. 96-104). Association for Computational Linguistics.

Kyosung Koo (2006). Effects of using corpora and online reference tools on foreign language writing: a study of Korean learners of English as a second language. PhD. dissertation, *University of Iowa*.

Lee, D. Y. (2001). Genres, registers, text types, domains and styles: Clarifying the concepts and nevigating a path through the BNC jungle.

Partington, A. (1998). *Patterns and meanings: Using corpora for English language research and teaching* (Vol. 2). John Benjamins Publishing.

Riehmann, P., Gruendl, H., Froehlich, B., Potthast, M., Trenkmann, M., & Stein, B. (2011, March). The NETSPEAK WORDGRAPH: Visualizing keywords in context. In *Pacific Visualization Symposium (PacificVis), 2011 IEEE* (pp. 123-130). IEEE.

Scott, M. (2004). WordSmith tools version 4.

The British National Corpus, version 3 (BNC XML Edition). 2007. *Distributed by Oxford University Computing Services on behalf of the BNC Consortium*. URL: http://www.natcorp.ox.ac.uk/

ThinkMap Inc. (2005). Thinkmap Visual Thesaurus. Available from http:// www.visualthesaurus.com

Tsuruoka, Y., Tateishi, Y., Kim, J. D., Ohta, T., McNaught, J., Ananiadou, S., & Tsujii, J. I. (2005). Developing a robust part-of-speech tagger for biomedical text. In *Advances in informatics* (pp. 382-392). Springer Berlin Heidelberg.

Wattenberg, M., & Viégas, F. B. (2008). The word tree, an interactive visual concordance. *Visualization and Computer Graphics, IEEE Transactions on*, *14*(6), 1221-1228.

Wood, J. (2001). Can software support children's vocabulary development.*Language Learning & Technology*, *5*(1), 166-201.

Yeh, Y., Liou, H. C., & Li, Y. H. (2007). Online synonym materials and concordancing for EFL college writing. Computer Assisted Language Learning, *20*(2), 131-152.

SPIED: Stanford Pattern-based Information Extraction and Diagnostics

Sonal Gupta **Christopher D. Manning**
Department of Computer Science
Stanford University
{sonal, manning}@cs.stanford.edu

Abstract

This paper aims to provide an effective interface for progressive refinement of pattern-based information extraction systems. Pattern-based information extraction (IE) systems have an advantage over machine learning based systems that patterns are easy to customize to cope with errors and are interpretable by humans. Building a pattern-based system is usually an iterative process of trying different parameters and thresholds to learn patterns and entities with high precision and recall. Since patterns are interpretable to humans, it is possible to identify sources of errors, such as patterns responsible for extracting incorrect entities and vice-versa, and correct them. However, it involves time consuming manual inspection of the extracted output. We present a light-weight tool, SPIED, to aid IE system developers in learning entities using patterns with bootstrapping, and visualizing the learned entities and patterns with explanations. SPIED is the first publicly available tool to visualize diagnostic information of multiple pattern learning systems to the best of our knowledge.

1 Introduction

Entity extraction using rules dominates commercial industry, mainly because rules are effective, interpretable by humans, and easy to customize to cope with errors (Chiticariu et al., 2013). Rules, which can be hand crafted or learned by a system, are commonly created by looking at the context around already known entities, such as surface word patterns (Hearst, 1992) and dependency patterns (Yangarber et al., 2000). Building a pattern-based learning system is usually a repetitive process, usually performed by the system developer, of manually examining a system's output to identify improvements or errors introduced by changing the entity or pattern extractor. Interpretability of patterns makes it easier for humans to identify sources of errors by inspecting patterns that extracted incorrect instances or instances that resulted in learning of bad patterns. Parameters range from window size of the context in surface word patterns to thresholds for learning a candidate entity. At present, there is a lack of tools helping a system developer to understand results and to improve results iteratively.

Visualizing diagnostic information of a system and contrasting it with another system can make the iterative process easier and more efficient. For example, consider a user trying to decide on the context's window size in surface words patterns. And the user deliberates that part-of-speech (POS) restriction of context words might be required for a reduced window size to avoid extracting erroneous mentions.[1] By comparing and contrasting extractions of two systems with different parameters, the user can investigate the cases in which the POS restriction is required with smaller window size, and whether the restriction causes the system to miss some correct entities. In contrast, comparing just accuracy of two systems does not allow inspecting finer details of extractions that increase or decrease accuracy and to make changes accordingly.

In this paper, we present a pattern-based entity learning and diagnostics tool, SPIED. It consists of two components: 1. pattern-based entity learning using bootstrapping (SPIED-Learn), and 2. visualizing the output of one or two entity learning systems (SPIED-Viz). SPIED-Viz is independent of SPIED-Learn and can be used with any pattern-based entity learner. For demonstration, we use the output of SPIED-Learn as an input to SPIED-

[1] A shorter context size usually extracts entities with higher recall but lower precision.

Proceedings of the Workshop on Interactive Language Learning, Visualization, and Interfaces, pages 38–44,
Baltimore, Maryland, USA, June 27, 2014. ©2014 Association for Computational Linguistics

Viz. SPIED-Viz has pattern-centric and entity-centric views, which visualize learned patterns and entities, respectively, and the explanations for learning them. SPIED-Viz can also contrast two systems by comparing the ranks of learned entities and patterns. In this paper, as a concrete example, we learn and visualize drug-treatment (DT) entities from unlabeled patient-generated medical text, starting with seed dictionaries of entities for multiple classes. The task was proposed and further developed in Gupta and Manning (2014b) and Gupta and Manning (2014a).

Our contributions in this paper are: 1. we present a novel diagnostic tool for visualization of output of multiple pattern-based entity learning systems, and 2. we release the code of an end-to-end pattern learning system, which learns entities using patterns in a bootstrapped system and visualizes its diagnostic output. The pattern learning code is available at `http://nlp.stanford.edu/software/patternslearning.shtml`. The visualization code is available at `http://nlp.stanford.edu/software/patternviz.shtml`.

2 Learning Patterns and Entities

Bootstrapped systems have been commonly used to learn entities (Riloff, 1996; Collins and Singer, 1999). SPIED-Learn is based on the system described in Gupta and Manning (2014a), which builds upon the previous bootstrapped pattern-learning work and proposed an improved measure to score patterns (Step 3 below). It learns entities for given classes from unlabeled text by bootstrapping from seed dictionaries. Patterns are learned using labeled entities, and entities are learned based on the extractions of learned patterns. The process is iteratively performed until no more patterns or entities can be learned. The following steps give a short summary of the iterative learning of entities belonging to a class DT:

1. Data labeling: The text is labeled using the class dictionaries, starting with the seed dictionaries in the first iteration. A phrase matching a dictionary phrase is labeled with the dictionary's class.

2. Pattern generation: Patterns are generated using the context around the positively labeled entities to create candidate patterns for DT.

3. Pattern learning: Candidate patterns are scored using a pattern scoring measure and the top ones are added to the list of learned patterns for DT. The maximum number of patterns learned is given as an input to the system by the developer.

4. Entity learning: Learned patterns for the class are applied to the text to extract candidate entities. An entity scorer ranks the candidate entities and adds the top entities to DT's dictionary. The maximum number of entities learned is given as an input to the system by the developer.

5. Repeat steps 1-4 for a given number of iterations.

SPIED provides an option to use any of the pattern scoring measures described in (Riloff, 1996; Thelen and Riloff, 2002; Yangarber et al., 2002; Lin et al., 2003; Gupta and Manning, 2014b). A pattern is scored based on the positive, negative, and unlabeled entities it extracts. The positive and negative labels of entities are heuristically determined by the system using the dictionaries and the iterative entity learning process. The oracle labels of learned entities are not available to the learning system. Note that an entity that the system considered positive might actually be incorrect, since the seed dictionaries can be noisy and the system can learn incorrect entities in the previous iterations, and vice-versa. SPIED's entity scorer is the same as in Gupta and Manning (2014a).

Each candidate entity is scored using weights of the patterns that extract it and other entity scoring measures, such as TF-IDF. Thus, learning of each entity can be explained by the learned patterns that extract it, and learning of each pattern can be explained by all the entities it extracts.

3 Visualizing Diagnostic Information

SPIED-Viz visualizes learned entities and patterns from one or two entity learning systems, and the diagnostic information associated with them. It optionally uses the oracle labels of learned entities to color code them, and contrast their ranks of correct/incorrect entities when comparing two systems. The oracle labels are usually determined by manually judging each learned entity as correct or incorrect. SPIED-Viz has two views: 1. a pattern-centric view that visualizes patterns of one

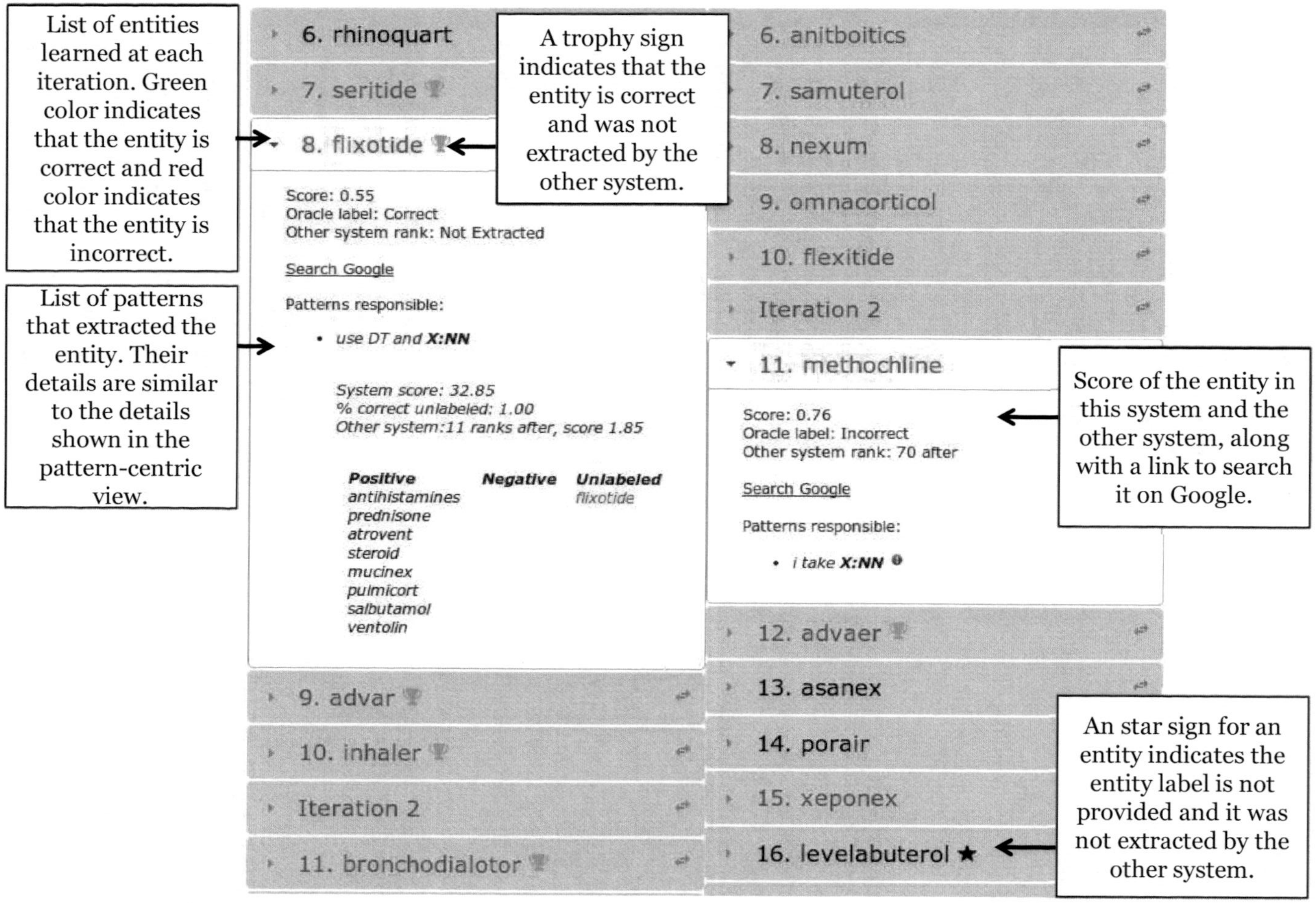

Figure 1: Entity centric view of SPIED-Viz. The interface allows the user to drill down the results to diagnose extraction of correct and incorrect entities, and contrast the details of the two systems. The entities that are not learned by the other system are marked with either a trophy (correct entity), a thumbs down (incorrect entity), or a star icon (oracle label missing), for easy identification.

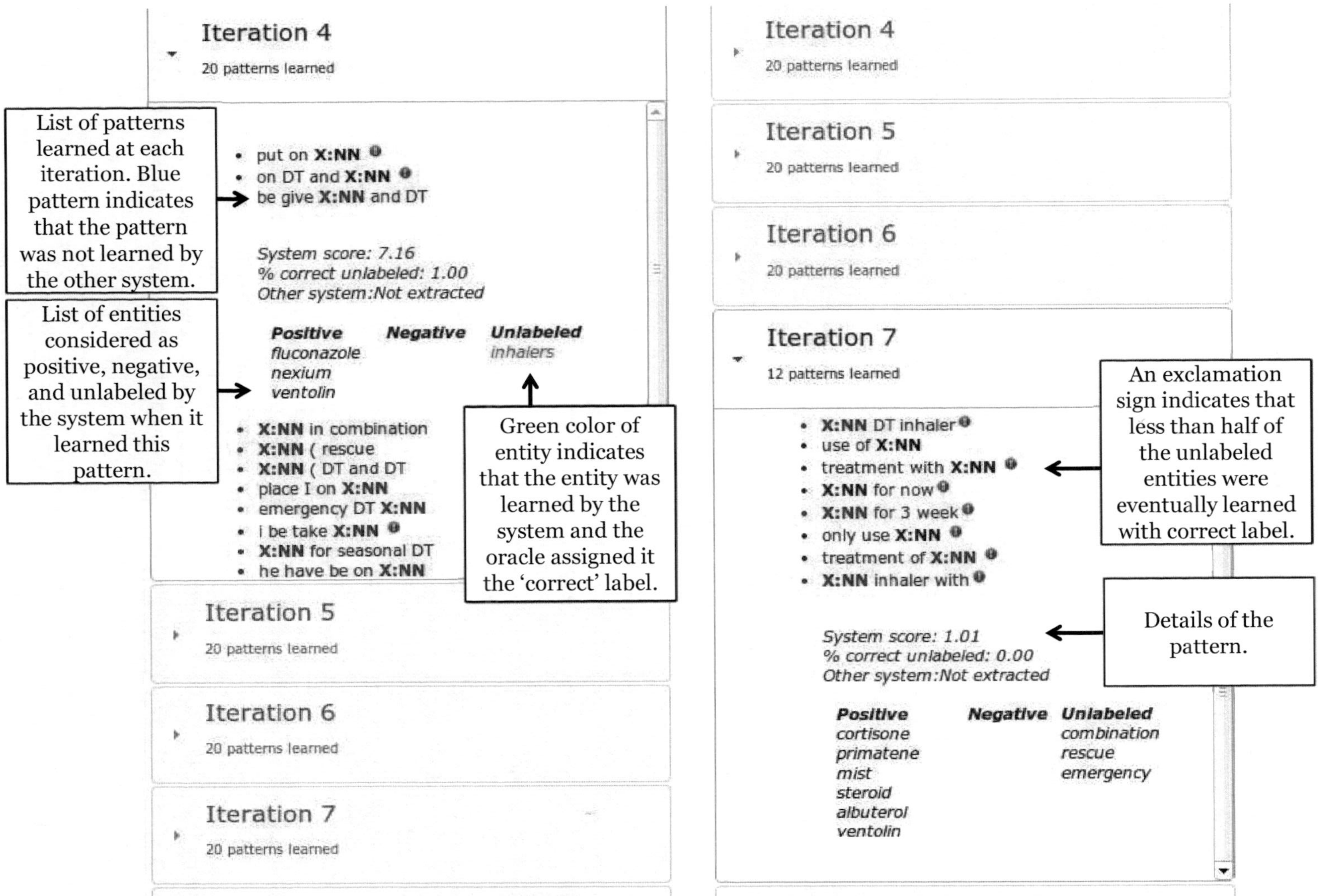

Figure 2: Pattern centric view of SPIED-Viz.

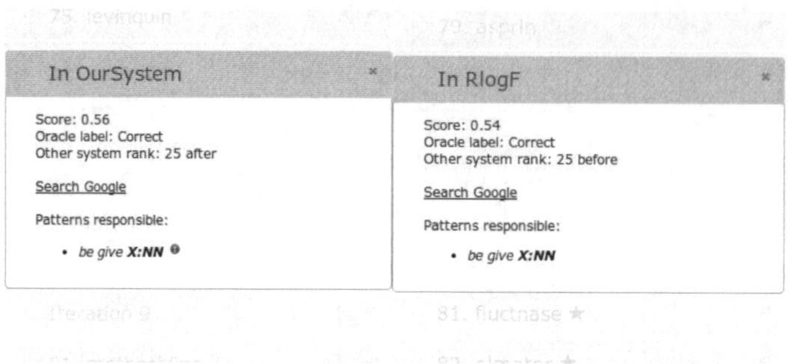

Figure 3: When the user click on the compare icon for an entity, the explanations of the entity extraction for both systems (if available) are displayed. This allows direct comparison of why the two systems learned the entity.

to two systems, and 2. an entity centric view that mainly focuses on the entities learned. Figure 1 shows a screenshot of the entity-centric view of SPIED-Viz. It displays following information:

Summary: A summary information of each system at each iteration and overall. It shows for each system the number of iterations, the number of patterns learned, and the number of correct and incorrect entities learned.

Learned Entities with provenance: It shows ranked list of entities learned by each system, along with an explanation of why the entity was learned. The details shown include the entity's oracle label, its rank in the other system, and the learned patterns that extracted the entity. Such information can help the user to identify and inspect the patterns responsible for learning an incorrect entity. The interface also provides a link to search the entity along with any user provided keywords (such as domain of the problem) on Google.

System Comparison: SPIED-Viz can be used to compare entities learned by two systems. It marks entities that are learned by one system but not by the other system, by either displaying a trophy sign (if the entity is correct), a thumbs down sign (if the entity is incorrect), or a star sign (if the oracle label is not provided).

The second view of SPIED-Viz is pattern-centric. Figure 2 shows a screenshot of the pattern-centric view. It displays the following information.

Summary: A summary information of each system including the number of iterations and number of patterns learned at each iteration and overall.

Learned Patterns with provenance: It shows ranked list of patterns along with the entities it extracts and their labels. Note that each pattern is associated with a set of positive, negative and unlabeled entities, which were used to determine its score.[2] It also shows the percentage of unlabeled entities extracted by a pattern that were eventually learned by the system and assessed as correct by the oracle. A smaller percentage means that the pattern extracted many entities that were either never learned or learned but were labeled as incorrect by the oracle.

Figure 3 shows an option in the entity-centric view when hovering over an entity opens a window on the side that shows the diagnostic information of the entity learned by the other system. This direct comparison is to directly contrast learning of an entity by both systems. For example, it can help the user to inspect why an entity was learned at an earlier rank than the other system.

An advantage of making the learning entities component and the visualization component independent is that a developer can use any pattern scorer or entity scorer in the system without depending on the visualization component to provide that functionality.

[2]Note that positive, negative, and unlabeled labels are different from the oracle labels, correct and incorrect, for the learned entities. The former refer to the entity labels considered by the system when learning the pattern, and they come from the seed dictionaries and the learned entities. A positive entity considered by the system can be labeled as incorrect by the human assessor, in case the system made a mistake in labeling data, and vice-versa.

4 System Details

SPIED-Learn uses TokensRegex (Chang and Manning, 2014) to create and apply surface word patterns to text. SPIED-Viz takes details of learned entities and patterns as input in a JSON format. It uses Javascript, angular, and jquery to visualize the information in a web browser.

5 Related Work

Most interactive IE systems focus on annotation of text, labeling of entities, and manual writing of rules. Some annotation and labeling tools are: MITRE's Callisto[3], Knowtator[4], SAPIENT (Liakata et al., 2009), brat[5], Melita (Ciravegna et al., 2002), and XConc Suite (Kim et al., 2008). Akbik et al. (2013) interactively helps non-expert users to manually write patterns over dependency trees. GATE[6] provides the JAPE language that recognizes regular expressions over annotations. Other systems focus on reducing manual effort for developing extractors (Brauer et al., 2011; Li et al., 2011). In contrast, our tool focuses on visualizing and comparing diagnostic information associated with pattern learning systems.

WizIE (Li et al., 2012) is an integrated environment for annotating text and writing pattern extractors for information extraction. It also generates regular expressions around labeled mentions and suggests patterns to users. It is most similar to our tool as it displays an explanation of the results extracted by a pattern. However, it is focused towards hand writing and selection of rules. In addition, it cannot be used to directly compare two pattern learning systems.

What's Wrong With My NLP?[7] is a tool for jointly visualizing various natural language processing formats such as trees, graphs, and entities. It can be used alongside our system to visualize the patterns since we mainly focus on diagnostic information.

6 Future Work and Conclusion

We plan to add a feature for a user to provide the oracle label of a learned entity using the interface. Currently, the oracle labels are assigned offline. We also plan to extend SPIED to visualize diagnostic information of learned relations from a pattern-based relation learning system. Another avenue of future work is to evaluate SPIED-Viz by studying its users and their interactions with the system. In addition, we plan to improve the visualization by summarizing the diagnostic information, such as which parameters led to what mistakes, to make it easier to understand for systems that extract large number of patterns and entities.

In conclusion, we present a novel diagnostic tool for pattern-based entity learning that visualizes and compares output of one to two systems. It is light-weight web browser based visualization. The visualization can be used with any pattern-based entity learner. We make the code of an end-to-end system freely available for research purpose. The system learns entities and patterns using bootstrapping starting with seed dictionaries, and visualizes the diagnostic output. We hope SPIED will help other researchers and users to diagnose errors and tune parameters in their pattern-based entity learning system in an easy and efficient way.

[3] `http://callisto.mitre.org`

[4] `http://knowtator.sourceforge.net`

[5] `http://brat.nlplab.org`

[6] `http://gate.ac.uk`

[7] `https://code.google.com/p/whatswrong`

References

Alan Akbik, Oresti Konomi, and Michail Melnikov. 2013. Propminer: A workflow for interactive information extraction and exploration using dependency trees. In *ACL (Conference System Demonstrations)*, pages 157–162.

Falk Brauer, Robert Rieger, Adrian Mocan, and Wojciech M. Barczynski. 2011. Enabling information extraction by inference of regular expressions from sample entities. In *CIKM*, pages 1285–1294.

Angel X. Chang and Christopher D. Manning. 2014. TokensRegex: Defining cascaded regular expressions over tokens. In *Stanford University Technical Report*.

Laura Chiticariu, Yunyao Li, and Frederick R. Reiss. 2013. Rule-based information extraction is dead! long live rule-based information extraction systems! In *Proceedings of the Conference on Empirical Methods in Natural Language Processing*, EMNLP '13, pages 827–832.

Fabio Ciravegna, Alexiei Dingli, Daniela Petrelli, and Yorick Wilks. 2002. User-system cooperation in document annotation based on information extraction. In *In Proceedings of the 13th International Conference on Knowledge Engineering and Knowledge Management, EKAW02*, pages 122–137. Springer Verlag.

Michael Collins and Yoram Singer. 1999. Unsupervised models for named entity classification. In *Proceedings of the Joint SIGDAT Conference on Empir-*

ical Methods in Natural Language Processing and Very Large Corpora, pages 100–110.

Sonal Gupta and Christopher D. Manning. 2014a. Improved pattern learning for bootstrapped entity extraction. In *Proceedings of the Eighteenth Conference on Computational Natural Language Learning (CoNLL)*.

Sonal Gupta and Christopher D. Manning. 2014b. Induced lexico-syntactic patterns improve information extraction from online medical forums. *Under Submission*.

Marti A Hearst. 1992. Automatic acquisition of hyponyms from large text corpora. In *Proceedings of the 14th International Conference on Computational linguistics*, COLING '92, pages 539–545.

Jin-Dong Kim, Tomoko Ohta, and Jun ichi Tsujii. 2008. Corpus annotation for mining biomedical events from literature. *BMC Bioinformatics*.

Yunyao Li, Vivian Chu, Sebastian Blohm, Huaiyu Zhu, and Howard Ho. 2011. Facilitating pattern discovery for relation extraction with semantic-signature-based clustering. In *Proceedings of the 20th ACM International Conference on Information and Knowledge Management*, CIKM '11, pages 1415–1424.

Yunyao Li, Laura Chiticariu, Huahai Yang, Frederick R. Reiss, and Arnaldo Carreno-fuentes. 2012. Wizie: A best practices guided development environment for information extraction. In *Proceedings of the ACL 2012 System Demonstrations*, ACL '12, pages 109–114.

Maria Liakata, Claire Q, and Larisa N. Soldatova. 2009. Semantic annotation of papers: Interface & enrichment tool (sapient). In *Proceedings of the BioNLP 2009 Workshop*, pages 193–200.

Winston Lin, Roman Yangarber, and Ralph Grishman. 2003. Bootstrapped learning of semantic classes from positive and negative examples. In *Proceedings of the ICML 2003 Workshop on The Continuum from Labeled to Unlabeled Data in Machine Learning and Data Mining*.

Ellen Riloff. 1996. Automatically generating extraction patterns from untagged text. In *Proceedings of the 13th National Conference on Artificial Intelligence*, AAAI'96, pages 1044–1049.

Michael Thelen and Ellen Riloff. 2002. A bootstrapping method for learning semantic lexicons using extraction pattern contexts. In *Proceedings of the Conference on Empirical Methods in Natural Language Processing*, EMNLP '02, pages 214–221.

Roman Yangarber, Ralph Grishman, and Pasi Tapanainen. 2000. Automatic acquisition of domain knowledge for information extraction. In *Proceedings of the 18th International Conference on Computational Linguistics*, COLING '00, pages 940–946.

Roman Yangarber, Winston Lin, and Ralph Grishman. 2002. Unsupervised learning of generalized names. In *Proceedings of the 19th International Conference on Computational Linguistics*, COLING '02.

Interactive Exploration of Asynchronous Conversations: Applying a User-centered Approach to Design a Visual Text Analytic System

Enamul Hoque, Giuseppe Carenini
{enamul,carenini}@cs.ubc.ca
Department of Computer Science
University of British Columbia
Vancouver, Canada

Shafiq Joty
sjoty@qf.org.qa
Qatar Computing Research Institute
Qatar Foundation
Doha, Qatar

Abstract

Exploring an online conversation can be very difficult for a user, especially when it becomes a long complex thread. We follow a human-centered design approach to tightly integrate text mining methods with interactive visualization techniques to support the users in fulfilling their information needs. The resulting visual text analytic system provides multifaceted exploration of asynchronous conversations. We discuss a number of open challenges and possible directions for further improvement including the integration of interactive human feedback in the text mining loop, applying more advanced text analysis methods with visualization techniques, and evaluating the system with real users.

1 Introduction

With the rapid adoption of Web-based social media, asynchronous online conversations are becoming extremely common for supporting communication and collaboration. An asynchronous conversation such as a blog may start with a news article or an editorial opinion, and later generate a long and complex thread as comments are added by the participants (Carenini et al., 2011). Consider a scenario, where a reader opens a blog conversation about Obama's healthcare policy. The reader wants to know why people are supporting or opposing *ObamaCare*. However, since some related discussion topics like *student loan* and *job recession* are introduced, the reader finds it hard to keep track of the comments about *ObamaCare*, which end up being buried in the long discussion. This may lead to an information overload problem, where the reader gets overwhelmed, starts to skip comments, and eventually leaves the conversation without satisfying her information needs (Jones et al., 2004).

How can we support the user in performing this and similar information seeking tasks? Arguably, supporting this task requires tight integration between Natural Language Processing (NLP) and information visualization (InfoVis) techniques, but what specific text analysis methods should be applied? What metadata of the conversation could be useful to the user? How this data should be visualized to the user? And even more importantly, how NLP and InfoVis techniques should be effectively integrated? Our hypothesis is that to answer these questions effectively, we need to apply human-centered design methodologies originally devised for generic InfoVis (e.g., (Munzner, 2009; Sedlmair et al., 2012)). Starting from an analysis of user behaviours and needs in the target conversational domain, such methods help uncover useful task and data abstractions that can guide system design. On the one hand, task and data abstractions can characterize the type of information that needs to be extracted from the conversation; on the other hand, they can inform the design of the visual encodings and interaction techniques. More tellingly, as both the NLP and the InfoVis components of the resulting system refer to a common set of task and data abstractions, they are more likely to be consistent and synergistic.

We have explored this hypothesis in developing ConVis, a visual analytic system to support the interactive analysis of blog conversations. In the first part of the paper, we describe the development of ConVis, from characterizing the domain of blogs, its users, tasks and data, to designing and implementing specific NLP and InfoVis techniques informed by our user-centered design. In the second part of the paper, starting from an informal evaluation of Convis and a comprehensive literature review, we discuss several ideas on how ConVis (and similar systems) could be further improved and tested. These include the integration of interactive human feedback in the text mining techniques

Proceedings of the Workshop on Interactive Language Learning, Visualization, and Interfaces, pages 45–52,
Baltimore, Maryland, USA, June 27, 2014. ©2014 Association for Computational Linguistics

(which are based on Machine Learning), the coupling of even more advanced NLP methods with the InfoVis techniques, and the challenges in running evaluations of ConVis and similar interfaces.

2 Related Work

While in the last decade, NLP and InfoVis methods have been investigated to support the user in making sense of conversational data, most of this work has been limited in several ways.

For example, earlier works on visualizing asynchronous conversations primarily investigated how to reveal the thread structure of a conversation using tree visualization techniques, such as using a mixed-model visualization to show both chronological sequence and reply relationships (Venolia and Neustaedter, 2003), thumbnail metaphor using a sequence of rectangles (Wattenberg and Millen, 2003; Kerr, 2003), and radial tree layout (Pascual-Cid and Kaltenbrunner, 2009). However, such visualizations did not focus on analysing the actual content (i.e., the text) of the conversations, which is something that according to our user-centred design users are very interested in.

On the other hand, text mining approaches that perform content analysis of the conversations, such as finding primary themes (or topics) within conversations (Sack, 2000; Dave et al., 2004), or visualizing the content evolution over time (Wei et al., 2010; Viégas et al., 2006), often did not derive their visual encodings and interactive techniques from task and data abstractions based on a detailed analysis of specific user needs and requirements in the target domains.

Furthermore, more on the technical side, the text analysis methods employed by these approaches are not designed to exploit the specific characteristics of asynchronous conversations (e.g., use of quotation). Recently, (Joty et al., 2013b) has shown that topic segmentation and labeling models are more accurate when these specific characteristics are taken into account. The methods presented in (Joty et al., 2013b) are adopted in ConVis.

In general, to the best of our knowledge, no previous work has applied user-centred design to tightly integrate text mining methods with interactive visualization in the domain of asynchronous conversations.

3 Domains and User Activities

Conversational domains: The phenomenal adoption of novel Web-based social media has lead to the rise of textual conversations in many different modalities. While email remains a fundamental way of communicating for most people, other conversational modalities such as blogs, microblogs (e.g., Twitter) and discussion fora have quickly become widely popular. Since the nature of data and tasks may vary significantly from one domain to the other, rather than trying to build an one-size-fit-all interface, we follow a design methodology that is driven by modeling the tasks and usage characteristics in a specific domain.

In this work, we focus on blogs, where people can express their thoughts and engage in online discussions. Due to the large number of comments with complex thread structure (Joty et al., 2013b), mining and visualizing blog conversations can become a challenging problem. However, the visualization can be effective for other threaded discussions (e.g., news stories, Youtube comments).

Users: As shown in Table 1, blog users can be categorized into two groups based on their activities: (a) *participants* who already contributed to the conversations, and (b) *non-participants* who wish to join the conversations or analyze the conversations. Depending on different user groups the tasks might vary as well, something that needs to be taken into account in the design process.

For example, imagine a participant who has expressed her opinion about a major political issue. After some time, she may become interested to know what comments were made supporting or opposing her opinion, and whether those comments require a reply right away. On the contrary, a non-participant, who is interested in joining the ongoing conversation on that particular political issue, may want to decide whether and how she should contribute by quickly skimming through a long thread of blog comments. Another group of users may include the analysts, a policy maker for instance, who does not wish to join the conversation, but may want to make an informed decision based on a summary of arguments used to support or oppose the political issue.

Once the conversation becomes inactive (i.e., no further comments are added), still a distinction may remain between the activities of participants and non-participants on tasks (see Table 1). In our work, we have initially concentrated on supporting

User types	Ongoing conversation	Inactive/past conversation
Participant	Already joined the conversation (wants to get updated and possibly make new comments)	Wants to delve into the past conversations and re-examine what was discussed, what she commented on, what other people replied, etc.
Non-participant	**Potential participant** (wants to join the conversation) **Analyst** (wants to analyze the ongoing conversation, but does not intend to join)	Wants to analyze and gain insight about the past conversation.

Table 1: User categorization for asynchronous conversation.

the non-participant's activity on an inactive conversation (as opposed to an ongoing conversation).

4 Designing ConVis: From Tasks to NLP and InfoVis Techniques

We now briefly describe our design approach for integrating text mining techniques with interactive visualization in ConVis. We first characterize the domain of blogs and perform the data and tasks abstraction according to the nested model of design study (Munzner, 2009). We then mine the data as appeared to be essential from that data and task analysis, followed by iteratively refining the design of ConVis that aims to effectively support the identified blog reading tasks (A more detailed analysis of the task abstractions and visual design is provided in (Hoque and Carenini, 2014)).

4.1 Tasks

To understand the blog reading tasks, we reviewed the literature focusing on why and how people read blogs. From the analysis, we found that the primary goals of reading blogs include information seeking, fact checking, guidance/opinion seeking, and political surveillance (Kaye, 2005). People may also read blogs to connect to their communities of interest (Dave et al., 2004; Mishne, 2006), or just for fun/ enjoyment (Baumer et al., 2008; Kaye, 2005).

Some studies have also revealed interesting behavioural patterns of blog readers. For example, people often look for variety of opinions and have tendencies to switch from one topic to another quickly (Singh et al., 2010; Munson and Resnick, 2010). In addition, they often exhibit exploratory behaviour, i.e., they quickly skim through a few posts about a topic before delving deeper into its details (Zinman, 2011). Therefore, the interface should facilitate open-ended exploration, by providing navigational cues that help the user to seek interesting comments.

From the analyses of primary goals of blog reading, we compile a list of tasks and the associated data variables that one would wish to visualize for these tasks. These tasks can be framed as a set of questions, for instance, 'what do people say about topic X?', 'how other people's viewpoints differ from my current viewpoint on topic X?', 'what are some interesting/funny comments to read?' We then identify the primary data variables involved in these tasks and their abstract types. For instance, most of these questions involve *topics* discussed and *sentiments* expressed in the conversation. Note that some questions may additionally require to know people-centric information and relate such information to the visualization design. We also identify a set of metadata to be useful cues for navigating a conversation (the position of the comments, thread structure, and comment length) (Narayan and Cheshire, 2010; Baumer et al., 2008). We choose to encode the *position of the comments* (ordinal) as opposed to their *timestamps* (quantitative); since the exact timestamp of a comment is less important to users than its chronological position with respect to the other comments (Baumer et al., 2008).

4.2 Text Analysis

Since most of the blog reading tasks we identified involved topics and sentiments expressed in the conversation, we applied both topic modeling and sentiment analysis on a given conversation.

In topic modeling, we group the sentences of a blog conversation into a number of topical clusters and label each cluster by assigning a short informative topic descriptor (i.e., a keyphrase). To find the topical clusters and their associated labels, we apply the topic segmentation and labeling models recently proposed by (Joty et al., 2013b) for asynchronous conversations, and successfully evaluated on email and blog datasets. More specifically, for topic segmentation, we use their best unsupervised topic segmentation model LCSeg+FQG, which extends the generic lexical cohesion based topic segmenter (LCSeg) (Galley et al., 2003)

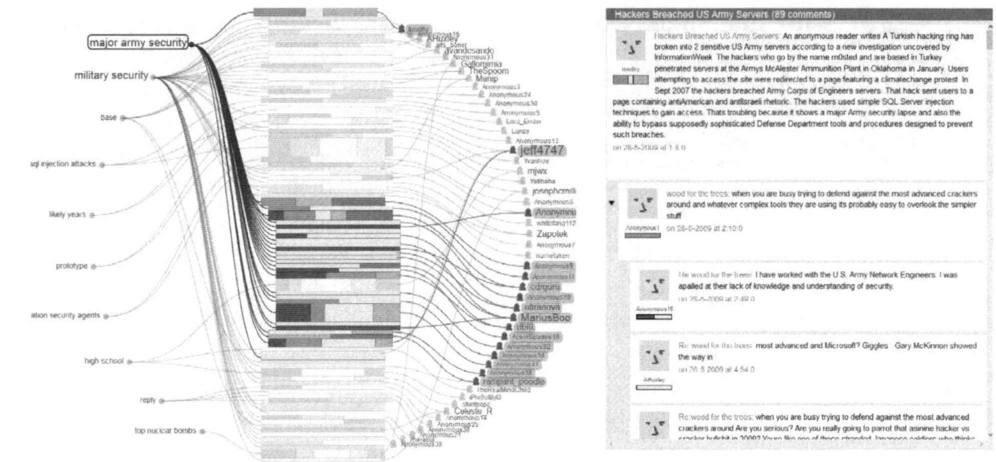

Figure 1: A snapshot of ConVis showing a blog conversation from Slashdot, where the user has hovered the mouse over a topic element ('major army security') that highlights the connecting visual links, brushing the related *authors*(right), and providing visual prominence to the related comments in the Thread Overview (middle).

to consider a fine-grain conversational structure of the conversation, i.e., the Fragment Quotation Graph (FQG) (Carenini et al., 2007). The FQG captures the reply relations between text fragments, which are extracted by analyzing the actual body of the comments, thus provides a finer representation of the conversation than the reply-to structure. Similarly, the topic labels are found by using their best unsupervised graph-based ranking model (i.e., BiasedCorank) that extracts representative keyphrases for each topical segment by combining informative clues from initial sentences of the segment and the fine-grain conversational structure, i.e., the FQG.

For sentiment analysis, we apply the Semantic Orientation CALculator (SO-CAL) (Taboada et al., 2011), which is a lexicon-based approach (i.e., unsupervised) for determining sentiment of a text. Its performance is consistent across various domains and on completely unseen data, thus making a suitable tool for our purpose. We define five different polarity intervals (-2 to +2), and for each comment we count how many sentences fall in any of these polarity intervals to compute the polarity distribution for that comment.

While designing and implementing ConVis, we have been mainly working with blog conversations from two different sources: Slashdot[1]— a technology related blog site, and Daily Kos[2]— a political analysis blog site.

4.3 Designing Interactive Visualization

Upon identifying the tasks and data variables, we design the visual encoding and user interactions. Figure 1 shows an initial prototype of ConVis. [3] It is designed as an overview + details interface, since it has been found to be more effective for text comprehension tasks than other approaches such as zooming and focus+context (Cockburn et al., 2008). The overview consists of what was discussed by whom (i.e., topics and authors) and a visual summary of the whole conversation (i.e., the Thread Overview), while the detailed view represents the actual conversation. The Thread Overview visually represents each comment of the discussion as a horizontal stacked bar, where each stacked bar encodes three different metadata (comment length, position of the comment in the thread, and depth of the comment within the thread). To express the sentiment distribution within a comment, the number of sentences that belong to a particular sentiment orientation is indicated by the width of each cell within a stacked bar. A set of five diverging colors was used to visualize this distribution in a perceptually meaningful order, ranging from purple (highly negative) to orange (highly positive). Thus, the distribution of colors in the Thread Overview can help the user to perceive the kind of conversation they are going to deal with. For example, if the Thread Overview is

[1] http://slashdot.org

[2] http://www.dailykos.com

[3] https://www.cs.ubc.ca/cs-research/lci/research-groups/natural-language-processing/ConVis.html

mostly in strong purple color, then the conversation has many negative comments.

The primary facets of the conversations, namely topics and authors are presented in a circular layout around the Thread Overview. Both topics and authors are positioned according to their chronological order in the conversation starting from the top, allowing the user to understand how the conversation evolves as the discussion progresses. The font size of facet items helps the user to quickly identify what are the mostly discussed themes and who are the most dominant participants within a conversation. Finally, the facet elements are connected to their corresponding comments in the Thread Overview via subtle curved links indicating topic-comment-author relationships. While a common way to relate various elements in multiple views is synchronized visual highlighting, we choose visual links to connect related entities. This was motivated by the findings that users can locate visually linked elements in complex visualizations more quickly and with greater subjective satisfaction than plain highlighting (Steinberger et al., 2011). Finally, the Conversation View displays the actual text of the comments in the discussion as a scrollable list. At the left side of each comment, the following metadata are presented: title, author name, photo, and a stacked bar representing the sentiment distribution (mirrored from Thread Overview).

Exploring Conversations: ConVis supports multi-faceted exploration of conversations through a set of lightweight interactions (Lam, 2008) that can be easily triggered without causing drastic modifications to the visual encoding. The user can explore interesting topics/ authors by hovering the mouse on them, which highlights the connecting curved links and related comments in the Thread Overview (see Figure 1). As such, one can quickly understand how multiple facet elements are related, which is useful for the tasks that require the user to interpret the relationships between facets. If the reader becomes further interested in specific topic/ author, she can subsequently click on it, resulting in drawing a thick vertical outline next to the corresponding comments in the Thread Overview. Such outlines are also mirrored in the Conversation View. Moreover, the user can select multiple facet items (for instance a topic and an author) to quickly understand who said about what topics.

Besides exploring by the topics/ authors, the reader can browse individual comments by hovering and clicking on them in the Thread Overview, that causes to highlight its topic and scrolling to the relevant comment in the Conversation View. Thus, the user can easily locate the comments that belong to a particular topic and/or author. Moreover, the keyphrases of the relevant topic and sentiments are highlighted in the Conversation View upon selection, providing more details on demand about what makes a particular comment positive/ negative or how it is related to a particular topic.

5 Further Challenges and Directions

After implementing the prototype, we ran an informal evaluation (Lam et al., 2012) with five target users (age range 18 to 24, 2 female) to evaluate the higher levels of the nested model (Munzner, 2009), where the aim was to collect anecdotal evidence that the system met its design goals. The participants' feedback from our evaluation suggests that ConVis can help the user to identify the topics and opinions expressed in the conversation; supporting the user in exploring comments of interest, even if they are buried near the end of the thread. We also identified further challenges from the observations and participants feedback. Based on our experience and literature review, we provide potential directions to address these challenges as we describe below.

5.1 Human in the Loop: Interactive Topic Revision

Although the topic modeling method we applied enhances the accuracy over traditional methods for non-conversational text, the informal evaluation reveals that still the extracted topics may not always match user's information need. In some cases, the results of topic modeling can mismatch with the reference set of topics/ concepts described by human (Chuang et al., 2013). Even the interpretations of topics can vary among people according to expertise and the current task in hand. In fact, during topic annotations by human experts, there was considerable disagreement on the number of topics and on the assignment of sentences to topic clusters (Joty et al., 2013b). Depending on user's mental model and current tasks, the topic modeling results may require to be more specific in some cases, and more generic in other cases. As such, the topic model needs to be revised based on user feedback to better support her analysis tasks. Thus, our goal is to support a human-in-the-loop topic modeling for asynchronous conversations via interactive visualization.

There have been some recent works for incorporating user supervision in probabilistic topic models (e.g., Latent Dirichlet Allocation (LDA)) by adding constraints in the form of must-link and cannot-link (Andrzejewski et al., 2009; Hu et al., 2011), or in the form of a one-to-one mapping between LDA's latent topics and user tags (Ramage et al., 2009). The feedback from users has been also integrated through visualizations, that steers a semi-supervised topic model (Choo et al., 2013).

In contrast to the above-mentioned methods that are designed for generic documents, we are focusing on how our topic modeling approach that is specific to asynchronous conversations, can be steered by the end-users. We are planning to combine a visual interface for expressing the user's intention via a set of actions, and a semi-supervised version of the topic model that can be iteratively refined from such user actions.

A set of possible topic revision operations are shown in Figure 2. Splitting a topic into further sub-topics can be useful when the user wants to explore the conversation at a finer-topic granularity (Figure 2(a)). A merging operation serves the opposite purpose, i.e., when the user wants to analyze the conversation at a coarser topic granularity (Figure 2(b)). Together, these two operations are intended to help the user in dynamically changing the granularity levels of different topics.

Since each topic is currently represented by a set of keyphrases, they can also be effectively used to revise the topic model. Consider an example, where the sentences related to two different keyphrases, namely 'Obama health policy' and 'job recession' are grouped together under the same topic. The user may realize that the sentences related to 'job recession' should have been separated from its original topic into a new one (Figure 2(c)). Finally, topic assignment modification can be performed, when the domain expert believes that a group of sentences are wrongly grouped/clustered (Figure 2(d)) by the system.

In order to design the interactive visualization and algorithms for incorporating user feedback, a number of open questions need to be answered. Some of these questions are related to the user requirement analysis of the problem domain, e.g., what are the tasks for exploring asynchronous conversation that require the introduction of user feedback to refine the topic model? What data should be shown to the user to help her decide what topic refinement actions are appropriate?

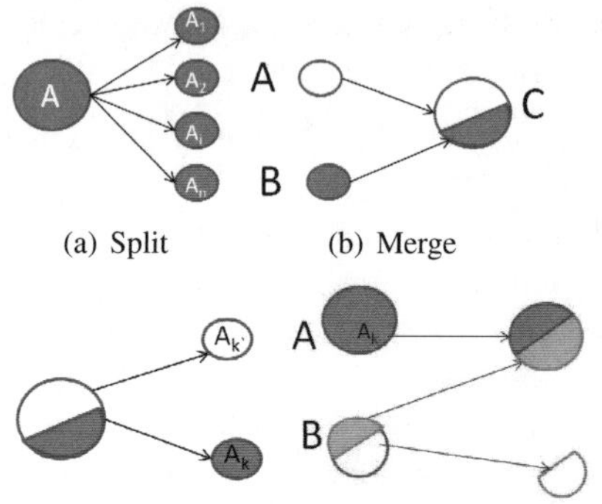

(a) Split (b) Merge (c) Create topic by a keyphrase (d) Topic assignment modification

Figure 2: Four different possible user actions for topic revision

In terms of designing the set of interaction techniques, the aim is to define a minimum set of model refinement operations, and allowing the user to express these operations from the visual interface in a way that enhances the ability to provide feedback. A domain expert could possibly express these operations through the direct manipulation method (e.g., dragging a topic node over another). A related open question is: how can we minimize the cognitive load associated with interpreting the modeling results and deciding the next round of topic revision operations?

From the algorithmic perspective, the most crucial challenge seems to be devising an efficient semi-supervised method in the current graph-based topic segmentation and labeling framework (Joty et al., 2013b). It needs to be fast enough to respond to the user refinement actions and update results in an acceptable period of time. In addition, determining the number of topics is a challenging problem when running the initial model and when splitting a topic further.

5.2 Coupling Advanced NLP Methods with Interactive Visualizations

In light of the informal evaluation, we also investigate how current NLP methods are supporting the tasks we identified and what additional methods could be incorporated? For example, one of the crucial data variable in most of the tasks is opinion. However, during the evaluation two users did not find the current sentiment analysis sufficient enough in revealing whether a comment is supporting/ opposing a preceding one. It seems that opinion seeking tasks (e.g., 'why people were supporting or opposing an opinion?') would require the reader to know the argumentation flow within the conversation, namely the rhetorical structure of each comment (Joty et al., 2013a) and how these structures are linked to each other.

An early work (Yee and Hearst, 2005) attempted to organize the comments using a treemap like layout, where the parent comment is placed on top as a text block and the space below the parent node is divided between supporting and opposing statements. We plan to follow this idea in ConVis, but incorporating a higher level discourse relation analysis of the conversations and detecting controversial topics.

Incorporating additional complex text analysis results into the visualization may require us to revisit some of the higher levels of the nested model, i.e., data abstraction and visual encoding. It may impose further tradeoffs for visual encoding; for instance how can we visually represent the argumentation structure within a conversation? How can we represent such structure, while preserving the data already found to be useful such as topic and thread structure? How can we represent that a topic is controversial? Besides text analysis results, some additional facets can become more useful to the participants (e.g., moderation scores, named entities), while an existing facet being less useful. In such cases, allowing the user to dynamically change the facets of interest can be useful.

5.3 Evaluation in the Wild

While controlled experiments allow us to measure the user performance on specific tasks for the given interface, they may not accurately capture real world uses scenario (Lam et al., 2012). In this context, an ecologically valid evaluation of ConVis would be to allow the users to use the system to read their own conversations of interest over an extended period of time. Such longitudinal study would provide valuable insights regarding the utility of the interface.

Evaluating the topic refinement approach for asynchronous conversation can be even more challenging. An initial approach could be to formulate some quantitative evaluation metrics, that help us understand whether the iterative feedback from the user would improve the resultant topic model in terms of agreement with the reference set of topics described by human annotators. However, such approach would not capture the subjective differences of the users in interpreting the topic model. It would be more interesting to see, how much users would actually care about providing the feedback to refine the model in a real world scenario? What refinement operations would be performed more often? Would these operations eventually support the user to perform some analysis tasks more effectively?

6 Conclusions

Understanding the user behaviours, needs, and requirements in the target domain is critical in effectively combining NLP and InfoVis techniques. In this paper, we apply a visualization design method (Munzner, 2009) to identify what information should be mined from the conversation as well as how the visual encoding and interaction techniques should be designed. We claim that the NLP and the InfoVis components of the resulting system, ConVis, are more consistent and better integrated, because they refer to a common set of task and data abstractions. In future work, we aim to explore a set of open challenges that were motivated by an initial informal evaluation of ConVis.

References

David Andrzejewski, Xiaojin Zhu, and Mark Craven. 2009. Incorporating domain knowledge into topic modeling via dirichlet forest priors. In *Proc. Conf. on Machine Learning*, pages 25–32.

Eric Baumer, Mark Sueyoshi, and Bill Tomlinson. 2008. Exploring the role of the reader in the activity of blogging. In *Proc. of CHI*, pages 1111–1120.

G. Carenini, R. T. Ng, and X. Zhou. 2007. Summarizing Email Conversations with Clue Words. In *Proc. conf. on World Wide Web*, pages 91–100.

Giuseppe Carenini, Gabriel Murray, and Raymond Ng. 2011. *Methods for Mining and Summarizing Text Conversations*. Morgan Claypool.

Jaegul Choo, Changhyun Lee, Chandan K Reddy, and Haesun Park. 2013. Utopian: User-driven topic modeling based on interactive nonnegative matrix factorization. *IEEE Trans. Visualization & Comp. Graphics*, 19(12):1992–2001.

Jason Chuang, Sonal Gupta, Christopher Manning, and Jeffrey Heer. 2013. Topic model diagnostics: Assessing domain relevance via topical alignment. In *Proc. Conf. on Machine Learning*, pages 612–620.

Andy Cockburn, Amy Karlson, and Benjamin B Bederson. 2008. A review of overview+ detail, zooming, and focus+ context interfaces. *ACM Computing Surveys (CSUR)*, 41(1):2.

Kushal Dave, Martin Wattenberg, and Michael Muller. 2004. Flash forums and forumreader: navigating a new kind of large-scale online discussion. In *Proc. ACM Conf. on CSCW*, pages 232–241.

Michel Galley, Kathleen McKeown, Eric Fosler-Lussier, and Hongyan Jing. 2003. Discourse segmentation of multi-party conversation. In *Proc. of ACL*, pages 562–569.

Enamul Hoque and Giuseppe Carenini. 2014. ConVis: A visual text analytic system for exploring blog conversations. *(Computer Graphic Forum (to appear))*.

Yuening Hu, Jordan Boyd-Graber, and Brianna Satinoff. 2011. Interactive topic modeling. In *Proc. of ACL*.

Quentin Jones, Gilad Ravid, and Sheizaf Rafaeli. 2004. Information overload and the message dynamics of online interaction spaces: A theoretical model and empirical exploration. *Information Systems Research*, 15(2):194–210.

Shafiq Joty, Giuseppe Carenini, Raymond Ng, and Yashar Mehdad. 2013a. Combining intra-and multi-sentential rhetorical parsing for document-level discourse analysis. In *Proc. of ACL*.

Shafiq Joty, Giuseppe Carenini, and Raymond T Ng. 2013b. Topic segmentation and labeling in asynchronous conversations. *Journal of Artificial Intelligence Research*, 47:521–573.

B. K. Kaye. 2005. Web side story: An exploratory study of why weblog users say they use weblogs. AEJMC Annual Conf.

Bernard Kerr. 2003. Thread arcs: An email thread visualization. In *IEEE Symposium on Information Visualization*, pages 211–218.

H. Lam, E. Bertini, P. Isenberg, C. Plaisant, and S. Carpendale. 2012. Empirical studies in information visualization: Seven scenarios. *IEEE Trans. Visualization & Comp. Graphics*, 18(9):1520–1536.

Heidi Lam. 2008. A framework of interaction costs in information visualization. *IEEE Trans. Visualization & Comp. Graphics*, 14(6):1149–1156.

Gilad Mishne. 2006. Information access challenges in the blogspace. In *Workshop on Intelligent Information Access (IIIA)*.

Sean A Munson and Paul Resnick. 2010. Presenting diverse political opinions: how and how much. In *Proc. of CHI*, pages 1457–1466.

Tamara Munzner. 2009. A nested model for visualization design and validation. *IEEE Trans. Visualization & Comp. Graphics*, 15(6):921–928.

S. Narayan and C. Cheshire. 2010. Not too long to read: The tldr interface for exploring and navigating large-scale discussion spaces. In *Hawaii Conf. on System Sciences (HICSS)*, pages 1–10.

Víctor Pascual-Cid and Andreas Kaltenbrunner. 2009. Exploring asynchronous online discussions through hierarchical visualisation. In *IEEE Conf. on Information Visualization*, pages 191–196.

Daniel Ramage, David Hall, Ramesh Nallapati, and Christopher D Manning. 2009. Labeled LDA: A supervised topic model for credit attribution in multi-labeled corpora. In *Proc. of EMNLP*, pages 248–256.

Warren Sack. 2000. Conversation map: an interface for very-large-scale conversations. *Journal of Management Information Systems*, 17(3):73–92.

Michael Sedlmair, Miriah Meyer, and Tamara Munzner. 2012. Design study methodology: reflections from the trenches and the stacks. *IEEE Trans. Visualization & Comp. Graphics*, 18(12):2431–2440.

Param Vir Singh, Nachiketa Sahoo, and Tridas Mukhopadhyay. 2010. Seeking variety: A dynamic model of employee blog reading behavior. *Available at SSRN 1617405*.

Markus Steinberger, Manuela Waldner, Marc Streit, Alexander Lex, and Dieter Schmalstieg. 2011. Context-preserving visual links. *IEEE Trans. Visualization & Comp. Graphics*, 17(12):2249–2258.

Maite Taboada, Julian Brooke, Milan Tofiloski, Kimberly Voll, and Manfred Stede. 2011. Lexicon-based methods for sentiment analysis. *Computational linguistics*, 37(2):267–307.

Gina Danielle Venolia and Carman Neustaedter. 2003. Understanding sequence and reply relationships within email conversations: a mixed-model visualization. In *Proc. of CHI*, pages 361–368.

Fernanda B Viégas, Scott Golder, and Judith Donath. 2006. Visualizing email content: portraying relationships from conversational histories. In *Proc. of CHI*, pages 979–988.

Martin Wattenberg and David Millen. 2003. Conversation thumbnails for large-scale discussions. In *extended abstracts on CHI*, pages 742–743.

Furu Wei, Shixia Liu, Yangqiu Song, Shimei Pan, Michelle X Zhou, Weihong Qian, Lei Shi, Li Tan, and Qiang Zhang. 2010. Tiara: a visual exploratory text analytic system. In *Proc. ACM Conf. on Knowledge Discovery and Data Mining*, pages 153–162.

Ka-Ping Yee and Marti Hearst. 2005. Content-centered discussion mapping. *Online Deliberation 2005/DIAC-2005*.

Aaron Robert Zinman. 2011. *Me, myself, and my hyperego: understanding people through the aggregation of their digital footprints*. Ph.D. thesis, MIT.

MUCK: A toolkit for extracting and visualizing semantic dimensions of large text collections

Rebecca Weiss
Stanford University
Stanford, CA, 94305
rjweiss@stanford.edu

Abstract

Users with large text collections are often faced with one of two problems; either they wish to retrieve a semantically-relevant subset of data from the collection for further scrutiny (needle-in-a-haystack) or they wish to glean a high-level understanding of how a subset compares to the parent corpus in the context of aforementioned semantic dimensions (forest-for-the-trees). In this paper, I describe MUCK[1], an open-source toolkit that addresses both of these problems through a distributed text processing engine with an interactive visualization interface.

1 Introduction

As gathering large text collections grows increasingly feasible for non-technical users, individuals such as journalists, marketing/communications analysts, and social scientists are accumulating vast quantities of documents in order to address key strategy or research questions. But these groups often lack the technical skills to work with large text collections, in that the conventional approaches they employ (content analysis and individual document scrutiny) are not suitable for the scale of the data they have gathered. Thus, users require tools with the capability to filter out irrelevant documents while drilling-down to the documents that they are most interested in investigating with closer scrutiny. Furthermore, they require the capability to then evaluate their subset in context, as the contrast in attributes between their subset and the full corpora can often address many relevant questions.

This paper introduces a work-in-progress: the development of a toolkit that aids non-technical users of large text collections by combining semantic search and semantic visualization methods. The purpose of this toolkit is two-fold: first, to ease the technical burden of working with large-scale text collections by leveraging semantic information for the purposes of filtering a large collection of text down to the select sample documents that matter most to the user; second, to allow the user to visually explore semantic attributes of their subset in comparison to the rest of the text collection.

Thus, this toolkit comprises two components:

1. a distributed text processing engine that decreases the cost of annotating massive quantities of text data for natural language information

2. an interactive visualization interface that enables exploration of the collection along semantic dimensions, which then affords subsequent document selection and subset-to-corpora comparison

The text processing engine is extensible, enabling the future development of plug-ins to allow for tasks beyond the included natural language processing tasks, such that future users can embed any sentence- or document-level task to their processing pipeline. The visualization interface is built upon search engine technologies to decrease search result latency to user requests, enabling a high level of interactivity.

2 Related work

The common theme of existing semantic search and semantic visualization methods is to enable the user to gain greater, meaningful insight into the structure of their document collections through the use of transparent, trustworthy methods (Chuang et al., 2012; Ramage et al., 2009). The desired insight can change depending on the intended task.

[1]Mechanical Understanding of Contextual Knowledge

Proceedings of the Workshop on Interactive Language Learning, Visualization, and Interfaces, pages 53–58,
Baltimore, Maryland, USA, June 27, 2014. ©2014 Association for Computational Linguistics

For some applications, users are understood to have a need to find a smaller, relevant subset of articles (or even a single article) in a vast collection of documents, which we can refer to as a needle-in-a-haystack problem. For others, users simply require the ability to gain a broad but descriptive summary of a semantic concept that describes these text data, which we can refer to as a forest-for-the-trees problem.

For example, marketers and social scientists often study news data, as the news constitute a vitally important source of information that guide the agendas of marketing strategy and inform many theories underlying social behavior. However, their interests are answered at the level of sentences or documents that contain the concepts or entities that they care about. This need is often not met through simple text querying, which can return too many or too few relevant documents and sentences. This is an example of a needle-in-a-haystack problem, which has been previously addressed through the application of semantic search (Guha et al., 2003). Much of the literature on semantic search, in which semantic information such as named entity, semantic web data, or simple document categories are added to the individual-level results of a simple query in order to bolster the relevance of resulting query hits. This type of information has proven to be useful in filtering out irrelevant content for a wide array of information retrieval tasks (Blanco et al., 2011; Pound et al., 2010; Hearst, 1999b; Hearst, 1999a; Liu et al., 2009; Odijk et al., 2012).

Remaining in the same narrative, once a subset of relevant documents has been created, these users may wish to see how the semantic characteristics of their subset contrast to the parent collection from which it was drawn. A marketer may have a desire to see how the tone of coverage in news related to their client's brand compares to the news coverage of other brands of a similar type. A social scientist may be interested to see if one news organization covers more politicians than other news organizations. This is an example of a forest-for-the-trees problem. This type of problem has been addressed through the application of semantic visualization, which can be useful for trend analysis and anomaly detection in text corpora (Fisher et al., 2008; Chase et al., 1998; Hearst and Karadi, 1997; Hearst, 1995; Ando et al., 2000).

The toolkit outlined in this paper leverages both of these techniques in order to facilitate the user's ability to gain meaningful insight into various semantic attributes of their text collection while also retrieving semantically relevant documents.

3 Overview of System From User Perspective

The ordering of a user's experience with this toolkit is as follows:

1. Users begin with a collection of unstructured text documents, which must be made available to the system (e.g., on a local or network drive or as a list of URLs for remote content)

2. Users specify the types of semantic detail relevant to their analysis (named entities, sentiment, etc.), and documents are then parsed, annotated, and indexed.

3. Users interact with the visualization in order to create the subset of documents or sentences they are interested in according to semantic dimensions of relevance

4. Once a view has been adequately configured using the visual feedback, users are able to retrieve the documents or sentences referenced in the visualization from the document store

Items 2 and 3 are further elaborated in the sections on the backend and frontend.

4 Backend

The distributed processing engine is driven by a task planner, which is a framework for chaining per-document tasks. As diagrammed in figure 1, the system creates and distributes text processing tasks needed to satisfy the user's level of semantic interest according to the dependencies between the various integrated third-party text processing libraries. Additionally, this system does not possess dependencies on additional third-party large-scale processing frameworks or message queueing systems, which makes this toolkit useful for relatively large (i.e. millions of documents) collections as it does not require configuration of other technologies beyond maintaining a document store[2] and a search index.

[2]http://www.mongodb.com

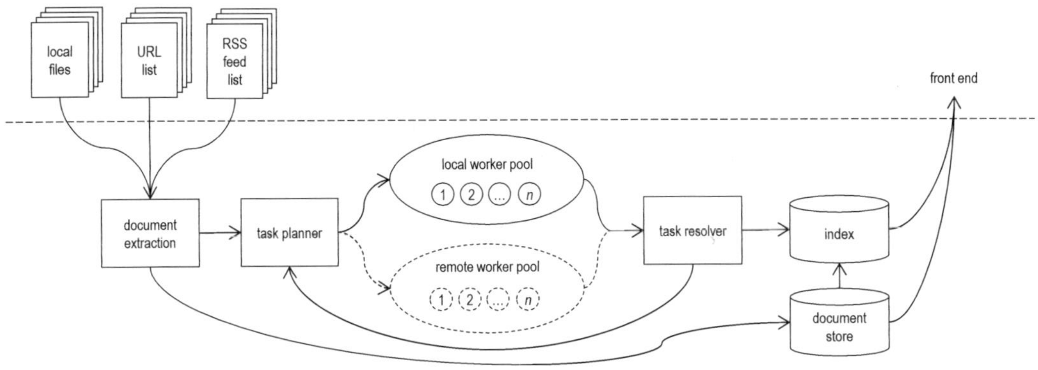

Figure 1: The architecture of the backend system.

Task planner and resolver system The semantic information extraction process occurs via defining a series of tasks for each document. This instantiates a virtual per-document queues of processing tasks. These queues are maintained by a task planner and resolver, which handles all of the distribution of processing tasks through the use of local or cloud resources[3]. This processing model enables non-technical users to describe a computationally-intensive, per-document processing pipeline without having to perform any technical configuration beyond specifying the level of processing detail output desired.

NLP task Currently, this system only incorporates the full Stanford CoreNLP pipeline[4], which processes each document into its (likely) constituent sentences and tokens and annotates each sentence and token for named entities, parts-of-speech, dependency relations, and sentiment (Toutanova et al., 2003; Finkel et al., 2005; De Marneffe et al., 2006; Raghunathan et al., 2010; Lee et al., 2011; Lee et al., 2013; Recasens et al., 2013; Socher et al., 2013). This extraction process is extensible, meaning that future tasks can be defined and included in the processing queue in the order determined by the dependencies of the new processing technology. Additional tasks at the sentence- or document-level, such as simple text classification using the Stanford Classifier (Manning and Klein, 2003), are included in the development roadmap.

[3]http://aws.amazon.com

[4]Using most recent version as of writing (v3.1)

5 Frontend

A semantic dimension of interest is mapped to a dimension of the screen as a context pane, as diagrammed in figure 2. Corpora-level summaries for each dimension are provided within each context pane for each semantic category, whereas the subset that the user interactively builds is visualized in the focus pane of the screen. By brushing each of semantic dimensions, the user can drill-down to relevant data while also maintaining an understanding of the semantic contrast between their subset and the parent corpus.

This visualization design constitutes a *multiple-view* system (Wang Baldonado et al., 2000), where a single conceptual entity can be viewed from several perspectives. In this case, the semantic concepts extracted from the data can be portrayed in several ways. This system maps semantic dimensions to visualization components using the following interaction techniques:

Navigational slaving Users must first make an initial selection for data by querying for a specific item of interest; a general text query (ideal for phrase matching), a named entity, or even an entity that served in a specific dependency relation (such as the dependent of an *nsubj* relation). This selection propagates through the remaining components of the interface, such that the remaining semantic dimensions are manipulated in the context of the original query.

Focus + Context Users can increase their understanding of the subset by zooming into a relevant

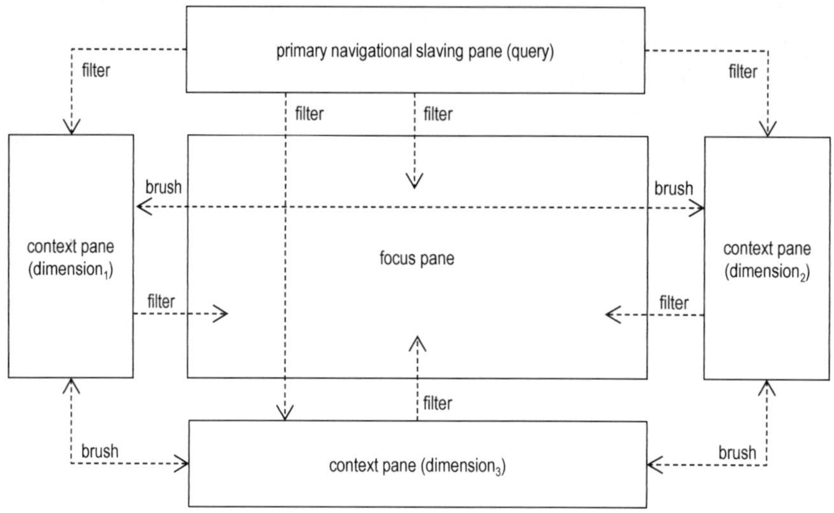

Figure 2: The wireframe of the frontend system.

selection in a semantic dimension (e.g. time).

Brushing Users can further restrict their subset by highlighting categories or ranges of interest in semantic dimensions (e.g. document sources, types of named entities). Brushing technique is determined by whether the semantic concept is categorical or continuous.

Filtering The brushing and context panes serve as filters, which restrict the visualized subset to only documents containing the intersection of all brushed characteristics.

This visualization design is enabled through the use of a distributed search engine[5], which enables the previously defined interactivity through three behaviors:

Filters Search engines enable the restriction of query results according to whether a query matches the parameters of a filter, such as whether a field contains text of a specific pattern.

Facets Search engines also can return subsets of documents structured along a dimension of interest, such as by document source types (if such information was originally included in the index).

Aggregations Aggregations allow for *bucketing* of relevant data and *metrics* to be calculated per bucket. This allows the swift retrieval of documents in a variety of structures, providing the hierarchical representation required for visualizing a subset along multiple semantic dimensions defined above.

Nesting All of these capabilities can be stacked upon each other, allowing for the multiple view system described above.

The visualization components are highly interactive, since the application is built upon a two-way binding design paradigm[6] between the DOM and the RESTful API of the index (Bostock et al., 2011).

6 Discussion and future work

This paper presents a work-in-progress on the development of a system that enables the extraction and visualization of large text collections along semantic dimensions. This system is open-source and extensible, so that additional per-document processing tasks for future semantic extraction procedures can be easily distributed. Additionally, this system does not possess requirements beyond maintaining a document store and a search index.

[5] http://www.elasticsearch.com

[6] http://www.angularjs.org

References

Rie Kubota Ando, Branimir K Boguraev, Roy J Byrd, and Mary S Neff. 2000. Multi-document summarization by visualizing topical content. In *Proceedings of the 2000 NAACL-ANLP Workshop on Automatic Summarization*, pages 79–98. Association for Computational Linguistics.

Roi Blanco, Harry Halpin, Daniel M Herzig, Peter Mika, Jeffrey Pound, Henry S Thompson, and T Tran Duc. 2011. Entity search evaluation over structured web data. In *Proceedings of the 1st international workshop on entity-oriented search workshop (SIGIR 2011), ACM, New York.*

Michael Bostock, Vadim Ogievetsky, and Jeffrey Heer. 2011. D^3 data-driven documents. *Visualization and Computer Graphics, IEEE Transactions on*, 17(12):2301–2309.

Penny Chase, Ray D'Amore, Nahum Gershon, Rod Holland, Rob Hyland, Inderjeet Mani, Mark Maybury, Andy Merlino, and Jim Rayson. 1998. Semantic visualization. In *ACL-COLING Workshop on Content Visualization and Intermedia Representation*.

Jason Chuang, Daniel Ramage, Christopher Manning, and Jeffrey Heer. 2012. Interpretation and trust: Designing model-driven visualizations for text analysis. In *Proceedings of the SIGCHI Conference on Human Factors in Computing Systems*, pages 443–452. ACM.

Marie-Catherine De Marneffe, Bill MacCartney, Christopher D Manning, et al. 2006. Generating typed dependency parses from phrase structure parses. In *Proceedings of LREC*, volume 6, pages 449–454.

Jenny Rose Finkel, Trond Grenager, and Christopher Manning. 2005. Incorporating non-local information into information extraction systems by gibbs sampling. In *Proceedings of the 43rd Annual Meeting on Association for Computational Linguistics*, pages 363–370. Association for Computational Linguistics.

Danyel Fisher, Aaron Hoff, George Robertson, and Matthew Hurst. 2008. Narratives: A visualization to track narrative events as they develop. In *Visual Analytics Science and Technology, 2008. VAST'08. IEEE Symposium on*, pages 115–122. IEEE.

Ramanathan Guha, Rob McCool, and Eric Miller. 2003. Semantic search. In *Proceedings of the 12th international conference on World Wide Web*, pages 700–709. ACM.

Marti A Hearst and Chandu Karadi. 1997. Cat-a-cone: an interactive interface for specifying searches and viewing retrieval results using a large category hierarchy. In *ACM SIGIR Forum*, volume 31, pages 246–255. ACM.

Marti A Hearst. 1995. Tilebars: visualization of term distribution information in full text information access. In *Proceedings of the SIGCHI conference on Human factors in computing systems*, pages 59–66. ACM Press/Addison-Wesley Publishing Co.

Marti A Hearst. 1999a. Untangling text data mining. In *Proceedings of the 37th annual meeting of the Association for Computational Linguistics on Computational Linguistics*, pages 3–10. Association for Computational Linguistics.

Marti A Hearst. 1999b. The use of categories and clusters for organizing retrieval results. In *Natural language information retrieval*, pages 333–374. Springer.

Heeyoung Lee, Yves Peirsman, Angel Chang, Nathanael Chambers, Mihai Surdeanu, and Dan Jurafsky. 2011. Stanford's multi-pass sieve coreference resolution system at the conll-2011 shared task. In *Proceedings of the Fifteenth Conference on Computational Natural Language Learning: Shared Task*, pages 28–34. Association for Computational Linguistics.

Heeyoung Lee, Angel Chang, Yves Peirsman, Nathanael Chambers, Mihai Surdeanu, and Dan Jurafsky. 2013. Deterministic coreference resolution based on entity-centric, precision-ranked rules.

Shixia Liu, Michelle X Zhou, Shimei Pan, Weihong Qian, Weijia Cai, and Xiaoxiao Lian. 2009. Interactive, topic-based visual text summarization and analysis. In *Proceedings of the 18th ACM conference on Information and knowledge management*, pages 543–552. ACM.

Christopher Manning and Dan Klein. 2003. Optimization, maxent models, and conditional estimation without magic. In *Proceedings of the 2003 Conference of the North American Chapter of the Association for Computational Linguistics on Human Language Technology: Tutorials-Volume 5*, pages 8–8. Association for Computational Linguistics.

Daan Odijk, Ork de Rooij, Maria-Hendrike Peetz, Toine Pieters, Maarten de Rijke, and Stephen Snelders. 2012. Semantic document selection. In *Theory and Practice of Digital Libraries*, pages 215–221. Springer.

Jeffrey Pound, Peter Mika, and Hugo Zaragoza. 2010. Ad-hoc object retrieval in the web of data. In *Proceedings of the 19th international conference on World wide web*, pages 771–780. ACM.

Karthik Raghunathan, Heeyoung Lee, Sudarshan Rangarajan, Nathanael Chambers, Mihai Surdeanu, Dan Jurafsky, and Christopher Manning. 2010. A multipass sieve for coreference resolution. In *Proceedings of the 2010 Conference on Empirical Methods in Natural Language Processing*, pages 492–501. Association for Computational Linguistics.

Daniel Ramage, Evan Rosen, Jason Chuang, Christopher D Manning, and Daniel A McFarland. 2009. Topic modeling for the social sciences. In *NIPS 2009 Workshop on Applications for Topic Models: Text and Beyond*, volume 5.

Marta Recasens, Marie-Catherine de Marneffe, and Christopher Potts. 2013. The life and death of discourse entities: Identifying singleton mentions. In *Proceedings of the 2013 Conference of the North American Chapter of the Association for Computational Linguistics: Human Language Technologies*, pages 627–633.

Richard Socher, Alex Perelygin, Jean Y Wu, Jason Chuang, Christopher D Manning, Andrew Y Ng, and Christopher Potts. 2013. Recursive deep models for semantic compositionality over a sentiment treebank. In *Proceedings of the Conference on Empirical Methods in Natural Language Processing (EMNLP)*, pages 1631–1642.

Kristina Toutanova, Dan Klein, Christopher D Manning, and Yoram Singer. 2003. Feature-rich part-of-speech tagging with a cyclic dependency network. In *Proceedings of the 2003 Conference of the North American Chapter of the Association for Computational Linguistics on Human Language Technology-Volume 1*, pages 173–180. Association for Computational Linguistics.

Michelle Q Wang Baldonado, Allison Woodruff, and Allan Kuchinsky. 2000. Guidelines for using multiple views in information visualization. In *Proceedings of the working conference on Advanced visual interfaces*, pages 110–119. ACM.

Design of an Active Learning System with Human Correction for Content Analysis

Nancy McCracken
School of Information Studies
Syracuse University, USA
njmccrac@syr.edu

Jasy Liew Suet Yan
School of Information Studies
Syracuse University, USA
jliewsue@syr.edu

Kevin Crowston
National Science Foundation
Syracuse University, USA
crowston@syr.edu

Abstract

Our research investigation focuses on the role of humans in supplying corrected examples in active learning cycles, an important aspect of deploying active learning in practice. In this paper, we discuss sampling strategies and sampling sizes in setting up an active learning system for human experiments in the task of content analysis, which involves labeling concepts in large volumes of text. The cost of conducting comprehensive human subject studies to experimentally determine the effects of sampling sizes and sampling sizes is high. To reduce those costs, we first applied an active learning simulation approach to test the effect of different sampling strategies and sampling sizes on machine learning (ML) performance in order to select a smaller set of parameters to be evaluated in human subject studies.

1 Introduction

Social scientists often use content analysis to understand the practices of groups by analyzing texts such as transcripts of interpersonal communication. Content analysis is the process of identifying and labeling conceptually significant features in text, referred to as "coding" (Miles and Huberman, 1994). For example, researchers studying leadership might look for evidence of behaviors such as "suggesting or recommending" or "inclusive reference" expressed in email messages. However, analyzing text is very labor-intensive, as the text must be read and understood by a human. Consequently, important research questions in the qualitative social sciences may not be addressed because there is too much data for humans to analyze in a reasonable time.

A few researchers have tried automatic techniques on content analysis problems. For example, Crowston *et al.* (2012) manually developed a classifier to identify codes related to group maintenance behavior in free/libre open source software (FLOSS) teams. Others have applied machine-learning (ML) techniques. For example, Ishita *et al.* (2010) used ML to automatically classify sections of text within documents on ten human values taken from the Schwartz's Value Inventory. Broadwell *et al.* (2012) developed models to classify sociolinguistic behaviors to infer social roles (e.g., leadership). On the best performing codes, these approaches achieve accuracies from 60–80%, showing the potential of automatic qualitative content analysis. However, these studies all limited their reports to a subset of codes used by the social scientists, due in part to the need for a large volume of training data.

The state-of-the-art ML approaches for content analysis require researchers to obtain a large amount of annotated data upfront, which is often costly or impractical. An active learning approach which uses human correction during the steps of active learning could potentially help produce a large amount of annotated data while minimizing the cost of human annotation effort. Unlike other text annotation tasks, the code annotation for content analysis requires significant cognitive effort, which may limit, or even nullify, the benefits of active learning.

We are building an active machine learning system to semi-automate the process of content analysis, and are planning to study the human role in such machine learning systems.

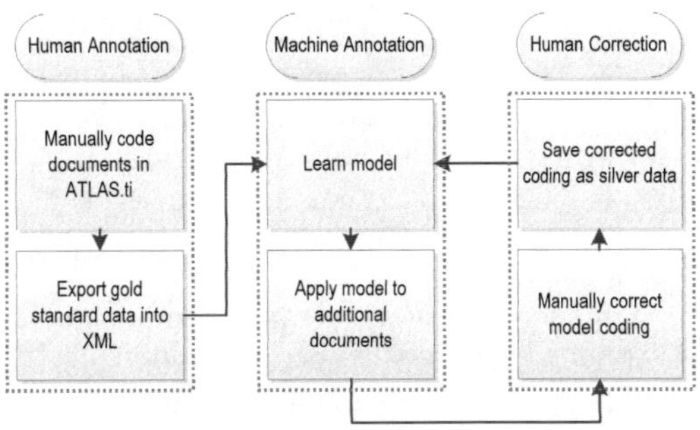

Figure 1. Active learning for semi-automatic content analysis.

As illustrated in Figure 1, the system design incorporates building a classifier from an initial set of hand-coded examples and iteratively improv-

Proceedings of the Workshop on Interactive Language Learning, Visualization, and Interfaces, pages 59–62,
Baltimore, Maryland, USA, June 27, 2014. ©2014 Association for Computational Linguistics

ing the model by having human annotators correct new examples identified by the system

Little is yet known about the optimal number of machine annotations to be presented to human annotators for correction, and how the sample sizes of machine annotations affect ML performance. Also, existing active learning sampling strategies to pick out the most "beneficial" examples for human correction to be used in the next round of ML training have not been tested in the context of social science data, where concept codes may be multi-dimensional or hierarchical, and the problem may be multi-label (one phrase or sentence in the annotated text has multiple labels). Also, concept codes tend to be very sparse in the text, resulting in a classification problem that has both imbalance—the non-annotated pieces of text (negative examples) tend to be far more frequent that annotated text—and rarity, where there may not be enough examples of some codes to achieve a good classifier.

The cost of conducting comprehensive human subject studies to experimentally determine the effects of sampling sizes and sampling sizes is high. Therefore, we first applied an active learning simulation approach to test the effect of different sampling strategies and sampling sizes on machine learning (ML) performance. This allows the human subject studies to involve a smaller set of parameters to be evaluated.

2 Related Work

For active learning in our system, we are using what is sometimes called pool-based active learning, where a large number of unlabeled examples are available to be the pool of the next samples. This type of active learning has been well explored for text categorization tasks (Lewis and Gale, 1994; Tong and Koller 2000; Schohn and Cohn 2000). This approach often uses the method of uncertainty sampling to pick new samples from the pool, both with probability models to give the "uncertainty" (Lewis and Gale, 1994) and with SVM models, where the margin numbers give the "uncertainty" (Tong and Koller 2000; Schohn and Cohn 2000). While much of the research focus has been on the sampling method, some has also focused on the size of the sample, e.g. in Schohn and Cohn (2000), sample sizes of 4, 8, 16, and 32 were used, where the result was that smaller sizes gave a steeper learning curve with a greater classification cost, and the authors settled on a sample size of 8. For additional active learning references, see the Settles (2009) survey of active learning literature.

This type of active learning has also been used in the context of human correction. One such system is described in Mandel *et al.* (2006), using active learning for music retrieval, where users were presented with up to 6 examples of songs to label. Another is the DUALLIST system described in Settles (2011) and Settles and Zhu (2012) where human experiments were carried out for text classification and other tasks. While most active learning experiments focus on reducing the number of examples to achieve an accurate model, there has been some effort to model the reduction of the cost of human time in annotation, where the human time is non-uniform per example. Both the systems in Culotta and McCallum (2005) and in Clancy *et al.* (2012) for the task of named entity extraction, modeled human cost in the context of sequential information extraction tasks. However, one difference between these systems and ours is that all of the tasks studied in these systems did not require annotators to have extensive training to annotate complex concept codes.

3 Problem

We worked with a pilot project in which researchers are studying leadership in open source software groups by analyzing open source developer emails. After a year of part-time annotation by two annotators, the researchers developed a codebook that provides a definition and examples for 35 codes. The coders achieved an inter-annotator agreement (kappa) of about 80%, and annotated about 400 email threads, consisting of about 3700 sentences. We used these coded messages as the "gold standard" data for our study. However, only 15 codes had more than 25 instances in the gold standard set. The most common code ("Explanation/Rationale/ Background") occurred only 319 times.

In our pilot correction experiments, annotators tried correcting samples of sizes ranging from about 50 to about 400. Anecdotal evidence indicates that annotators liked to annotate sample sizes of about 100 in order to achieve good focus on a particular code definition at one time, but without getting stressed with too many examples. Part of the required focus is that annotators need to refresh their memory on any particular code at the start of annotation, so switching frequently between different codes is cognitively taxing. This desired sample size contrasts with prior active learning systems that employ much smaller sample sizes, in the range of 1 to 20.

We are currently in the process of setting up the human experiments to test our main research question of achieving an accurate model for content analysis using a minimum of human effort.

In this paper, we discuss two questions for active learning in order to have annotators correct an acceptable number of machine annotations that are most likely to increase the performance of the ML model in each iteration. These are: how do different sample sizes and different sampling strategies of machine annotations presented to human annotators for correction in each round affect ML performance?

4 Active Learning Simulation Setup

In a similar strategy to that of Clancy *et al.* (2012), we carried out a preliminary investigation by conducting an active learning simulation on our gold standard data. The simulation starts with a small initial sample, and uses active learning where we "correct" the sample labels by taking labels from the gold standard corpus. For our simulation experiments, we separated the gold standard data randomly into a training set of 90% of the examples, 3298 sentences, and a test set of 10%, 366 sentences.

In the experimental setup, we used a version of libSVM that was modified to produce numbers of distance to the margin of the SVM classification. We implemented the multi-label classification by classifying each label separately where some sentences have the selected label and all others were counted as "negative" labels. We used svm weights to handle the problem of imbalance in the negative examples. After experimentation with different combinations of features, we used a set of features that was best overall for the codes: unigram tokens lowercased and filtered by stop words, bigrams, orthographic features from capitalization, the token count, and the role of the sender of the email.

For an initial sample, we randomly chose 3 positive and 3 negative examples from the development set to be the initial training set used for all experimental runs. We carried out experiments with a number of sample sizes, *b*, ranging over 5, 10, 20, 40, 50, 60, 80 and 100 instances.

For experiments on methods used to select correction examples, we have chosen to experiment with sampling methods similar to those found in Lewis and Gale (1994) and Lewis (1995) using a *random sampling method*, where a new sample is chosen randomly from the remaining examples in the development set, a *relevance sampling method*, where a new sample is chosen as the *b* number of most likely labeled candidates in the development set with the largest distance from the margin of the SVM classification, and an *uncertainty sampling method*, where a new sample is chosen as the *b* number of candidates in the region of uncertainty on either side of the margin of the SVM classification.

5 Preliminary Results

In this simulation experiment, the pool size is quite small (3664 examples) compared to the large amount of unlabeled data that is normally available for active learning, and would be available for our system under actual use. We tested the active learning simulation on 8 codes. There was no clear winning sampling strategy out of the 3 we used in the simulation experiment but random sampling (5 out of 8 codes) appeared to be the one that most often produced the highest $F_{\beta 2}$ score in the shortest number of iterations. Figure 2 shows the $F_{\beta 2}$ score for each sampling strategy based on code "Opinion/Preference" using sample sizes 5 and 100 respectively.

As for sampling sizes, we did not observe a large difference in the evolution of the $F_{\beta 2}$ score between the various sample sizes, and the learning curves in Figure 2, shown for the sample sizes of 5 and 100, are typical. This means that we should be able to use larger sample sizes for human subject studies to achieve the same improvements in performance as with the smaller sample sizes, and can carry out the experiments to relate the cost of human annotation with increases in performance.

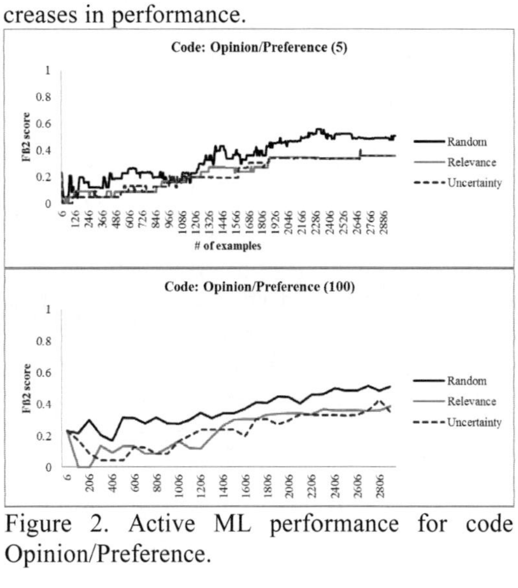

Figure 2. Active ML performance for code Opinion/Preference.

6 Conclusion and Future Work

Our findings are inconclusive as we have yet to run the active learning simulations on all the codes. However, preliminary results are directing us towards using larger sample sizes and then experimenting with random and uncertainty sampling in the human subject studies.

From our experiments with the different codes, we found the performance on less frequent codes to be problematic as it is difficult for the active learning system to identify potential positive examples to improve the models. While the system performance may improve to handle such sparse cases, it may be better to modify the codebook instead. We plan to give the user feedback on the performance of the codes at each iteration of the active learning and support modifications to the codebook, for example, the user may wish to drop some codes or collapse them according to some hierarchy. After all, if a code is not found in the text, it is hard to argue for its theoretical importance.

We are currently completing the design of the parameters of the active learning process for the human correction experiments on our pilot project with the codes about leadership in open source software groups. We will also be testing and undergoing further development of the user interface for the annotators.

Our next step will be to test the system on other projects with other researchers. We hope to gain more insight into what types of coding schemes and codes are easier to learn than others, and to be able to guide social scientists into developing coding schemes that are not only based on the social science theory but also useful in practice to develop an accurate classifier for very large amounts of digital text.

Acknowledgements:

This material is based upon work supported by the National Science Foundation under Grant No. IIS-1111107. Kevin Crowston is supported by the National Science Foundation. Any opinions, findings, and conclusions or recommendations expressed in this material are those of the author(s) and do not necessarily reflect the views of the National Science Foundation. The authors gratefully acknowledge helpful suggestions by the reviewers.

Reference

Broadwell, G. A., Stromer-Galley, J., Strzalkowski, T., Shaikh, S., Taylor, S., Liu, T., Boz, U., Elia, A., Jiao, L., & Webb, N. (2013). Modeling sociocultural phenomena in discourse. *Natural Language Engineering*, *19*(02), 213–257.

Clancy, S., Bayer, S. and Kozierok, R. (2012) "Active Learning with a Human In The Loop," Mitre Corporation.

Crowston, K., Allen, E. E., & Heckman, R. (2012). Using natural language processing technology for qualitative data analysis. *International Journal of Social Research Methodology*, *15*(6), 523–543.

Culotta, A. and McCallum, A. (2005) "Reducing Labeling Effort for Structured Prediction Tasks."

Ishita, E., Oard, D. W., Fleischmann, K. R., Cheng, A.-S., & Templeton, T. C. (2010). Investigating multi-label classification for human values. *Proceedings of the American Society for Information Science and Technology*, *47*(1), 1–4.

Miles, M. B., & Huberman, A. M. (1994). *Qualitative data analysis: An expanded sourcebook*. Sage Publications.

Lewis, D. D., & Gale, W. A. (1994). A sequential algorithm for training text classifiers. In *Proceedings of the 17th annual international ACM SIGIR conference on Research and development in information retrieval* (pp. 3-12).

Lewis, D. D. (1995). A sequential algorithm for training text classifiers: Corrigendum and additional data. In *ACM SIGIR Forum* (Vol. 29, No. 2, pp. 13-19).

Mandel, M. I., Poliner, G. E., & Ellis, D. P. (2006). Support vector machine active learning for music retrieval. *Multimedia systems*, *12*(1), 3-13.

Schohn, G., & Cohn, D. (2000). Less is more: Active learning with support vector machines. In *International Conference on Machine Learning* (pp. 839-846).

Settles, B. (2010). Active learning literature survey. *University of Wisconsin, Madison*, *52*, 55-66.

Settles, B. (2011). Closing the loop: Fast, interactive semi-supervised annotation with queries on features and instances. In *Proceedings of the Conference on Empirical Methods in Natural Language Processing* (pp. 1467-1478).

Settles, B., & Zhu, X. (2012). Behavioral factors in interactive training of text classifiers. In *Proceedings of the 2012 Conference of the North American Chapter of the Association for Computational Linguistics: Human Language Technologies* (pp. 563-567).

Tong, S., & Koller, D. (2002). Support vector machine active learning with applications to text classification. *The Journal of Machine Learning Research*, *2*, 45-66.

`LDAvis`: A method for visualizing and interpreting topics

Carson Sievert
Iowa State University
3414 Snedecor Hall
Ames, IA 50014, USA
cpsievert1@gmail.com

Kenneth E. Shirley
AT&T Labs Research
33 Thomas Street, 26th Floor
New York, NY 10007, USA
kshirley@research.att.com

Abstract

We present `LDAvis`, a web-based interactive visualization of topics estimated using Latent Dirichlet Allocation that is built using a combination of R and D3. Our visualization provides a global view of the topics (and how they differ from each other), while at the same time allowing for a deep inspection of the terms most highly associated with each individual topic. First, we propose a novel method for choosing which terms to present to a user to aid in the task of topic interpretation, in which we define the *relevance* of a term to a topic. Second, we present results from a user study that suggest that ranking terms purely by their probability under a topic is suboptimal for topic interpretation. Last, we describe `LDAvis`, our visualization system that allows users to flexibly explore topic-term relationships using relevance to better understand a fitted LDA model.

1 Introduction

Recently much attention has been paid to visualizing the output of topic models fit using Latent Dirichlet Allocation (LDA) (Gardner et al., 2010; Chaney and Blei, 2012; Chuang et al., 2012b; Gretarsson et al., 2011). Such visualizations are challenging to create because of the high dimensionality of the fitted model – LDA is typically applied to many thousands of documents, which are modeled as mixtures of dozens (or hundreds) of topics, which themselves are modeled as distributions over thousands of terms (Blei et al., 2003; Griffiths and Steyvers, 2004). The most promising basic technique for creating LDA visualizations that are both compact and thorough is *interactivity*.

We introduce an interactive visualization system that we call `LDAvis` that attempts to answer a few basic questions about a fitted topic model: (1) What is the meaning of each topic?, (2) How prevalent is each topic?, and (3) How do the topics relate to each other? Different visual components answer each of these questions, some of which are original, and some of which are borrowed from existing tools.

Our visualization (illustrated in Figure 1) has two basic pieces. First, the left panel of our visualization presents a global view of the topic model, and answers questions 2 and 3. In this view, we plot the topics as circles in the two-dimensional plane whose centers are determined by computing the distance between topics, and then by using multidimensional scaling to project the intertopic distances onto two dimensions, as is done in (Chuang et al., 2012a). We encode each topic's overall prevalence using the areas of the circles, where we sort the topics in decreasing order of prevalence.

Second, the right panel of our visualization depicts a horizontal barchart whose bars represent the individual terms that are the most useful for interpreting the currently selected topic on the left, and allows users to answer question 1, "What is the meaning of each topic?". A pair of overlaid bars represent both the corpus-wide frequency of a given term as well as the topic-specific frequency of the term, as in (Chuang et al., 2012b).

The left and right panels of our visualization are linked such that selecting a topic (on the left) reveals the most useful terms (on the right) for interpreting the selected topic. In addition, selecting a term (on the right) reveals the conditional distribution over topics (on the left) for the selected term. This kind of linked selection allows users to examine a large number of topic-term relationships in a compact manner.

A key innovation of our system is how we determine the most useful terms for interpreting a given topic, and how we allow users to interactively ad-

Proceedings of the Workshop on Interactive Language Learning, Visualization, and Interfaces, pages 63–70,
Baltimore, Maryland, USA, June 27, 2014. ©2014 Association for Computational Linguistics

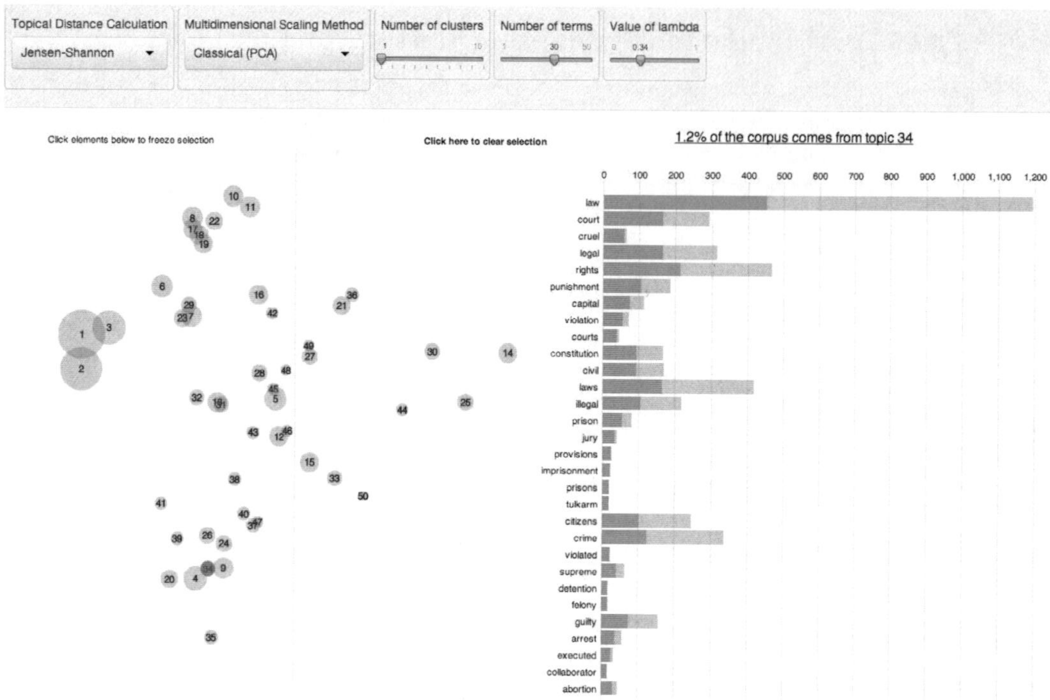

Figure 1: The layout of `LDAvis`, with the global topic view on the left, and the term barcharts (with Topic 34 selected) on the right. Linked selections allow users to reveal aspects of the topic-term relationships compactly.

just this determination. A topic in LDA is a multinomial distribution over the (typically thousands of) terms in the vocabulary of the corpus. To interpret a topic, one typically examines a ranked list of the most probable terms in that topic, using anywhere from three to thirty terms in the list. The problem with interpreting topics this way is that common terms in the corpus often appear near the top of such lists for multiple topics, making it hard to differentiate the meanings of these topics.

Bischof and Airoldi (2012) propose ranking terms for a given topic in terms of both the *frequency* of the term under that topic as well as the term's *exclusivity* to the topic, which accounts for the degree to which it appears in that particular topic to the exclusion of others. We propose a similar measure that we call the *relevance* of a term to a topic that allows users to flexibly rank terms in order of usefulness for interpreting topics. We discuss our definition of relevance, and its graphical interpretation, in detail in Section 3.1. We also present the results of a user study conducted to determine the optimal tuning parameter in the definition of relevance to aid the task of topic interpretation in Section 3.2, and we describe how we incorporate relevance into our interactive visualization in Section 4.

2 Related Work

Much work has been done recently regarding the interpretation of topics (i.e. measuring topic "coherence") as well as visualization of topic models.

2.1 Topic Interpretation and Coherence

It is well-known that the topics inferred by LDA are not always easily interpretable by humans. Chang et al. (2009) established via a large user study that standard quantitative measures of fit, such as those summarized by Wallach et al. (2009), do not necessarily agree with measures of topic interpretability by humans. Ramage et al. (2009) assert that "characterizing topics is hard" and describe how using the top-k terms for a given topic might not always be best, but offer few concrete alternatives.

AlSumait et al. (2009), Mimno et al. (2011), and Chuang et al. (2013b) develop quantitative methods for measuring the interpretability of topics based on experiments with data sets that come with some notion of topical ground truth, such as document metadata or expert-created topic labels. These methods are useful for understanding, in a global sense, which topics are interpretable (and why), but they don't specifically attempt to aid the user in interpreting *individual* topics.

Blei and Lafferty (2009) developed "Turbo Topics", a method of identifying n-grams within LDA-inferred topics that, when listed in decreasing order of probability, provide users with extra information about the usage of terms within topics. This two-stage process yields good results on experimental data, although the resulting output is still simply a ranked list containing a mixture of terms and n-grams, and the usefulness of the method for topic interpretation was not tested in a user study.

Newman et al. (2010) describe a method for ranking terms within topics to aid interpretability called Pointwise Mutual Information (PMI) ranking. Under PMI ranking of terms, each of the ten most probable terms within a topic are ranked in decreasing order of approximately how often they occur in close proximity to the nine other most probable terms from that topic in some large, external "reference" corpus, such as Wikipedia or Google n-grams. Although this method correlated highly with human judgments of term importance within topics, it does not easily generalize to topic models fit to corpora that don't have a readily available external source of word co-occurrences.

In contrast, Taddy (2011) uses an intrinsic measure to rank terms within topics: a quantity called *lift*, defined as the ratio of a term's probability within a topic to its marginal probability across the corpus. This generally decreases the rankings of globally frequent terms, which can be helpful. We find that it can be noisy, however, by giving high rankings to very rare terms that occur in only a single topic, for instance. While such terms may contain useful topical content, if they are very rare the topic may remain difficult to interpret.

Finally, Bischof and Airoldi (2012) develop and implement a new statistical topic model that infers both a term's frequency as well as its *exclusivity* – the degree to which its occurrences are limited to only a few topics. They introduce a univariate measure called a FREX score ("**FR**equency and **EX**clusivity") which is a weighted harmonic mean of a term's rank within a given topic with respect to frequency and exclusivity, and they recommend it as a way to rank terms to aid topic interpretation. We propose a similar method that is a weighted average of the logarithms of a term's probability and its lift, and we justify it with a user study and incorporate it into our interactive visualization.

2.2 Topic Model Visualization Systems

A number of visualization systems for topic models have been developed in recent years. Several of them focus on allowing users to browse documents, topics, and terms to learn about the relationships between these three canonical topic model units (Gardner et al., 2010; Chaney and Blei, 2012; Snyder et al., 2013). These browsers typically use lists of the most probable terms within topics to summarize the topics, and the visualization elements are limited to barcharts or word clouds of term probabilities for each topic, pie charts of topic probabilities for each document, and/or various barcharts or scatterplots related to document metadata. Although these tools can be useful for browsing a corpus, we seek a more compact visualization, with the more narrow focus of quickly and easily understanding the individual topics themselves (without necessarily visualizing documents).

Chuang et al. (2012b) develop such a tool, called "Termite", which visualizes the set of topic-term distributions estimated in LDA using a matrix layout. The authors introduce two measures of the usefulness of terms for understanding a topic model: *distinctiveness* and *saliency*. These quantities measure how much information a term conveys about topics by computing the Kullback-Liebler divergence between the distribution of topics given the term and the marginal distribution of topics (distinctiveness), optionally weighted by the term's overall frequency (saliency). The authors recommend saliency as a thresholding method for selecting which terms are included in the visualization, and they further use a seriation method for ordering the most salient terms to highlight differences between topics.

Termite is a compact, intuitive interactive visualization of the topics in a topic model, but by only including terms that rank high in saliency or distinctiveness, which are *global* properties of terms, it is restricted to providing a *global* view of the model, rather than allowing a user to deeply inspect individual topics by visualizing a potentially different set of terms for every single topic. In fact, Chuang et al. (2013a) describe the use of a "topic-specific word ordering" as potentially useful future work.

3 Relevance of terms to topics

Here we define *relevance*, our method for ranking terms within topics, and we describe the results of a user study to learn an optimal tuning parameter in the computation of relevance.

3.1 Definition of Relevance

Let ϕ_{kw} denote the probability of term $w \in \{1, ..., V\}$ for topic $k \in \{1, ..., K\}$, where V denotes the number of terms in the vocabulary, and let p_w denote the marginal probability of term w in the corpus. One typically estimates ϕ in LDA using Variational Bayes methods or Collapsed Gibbs Sampling, and p_w from the empirical distribution of the corpus (optionally smoothed by including prior weights as pseudo-counts).

We define the *relevance* of term w to topic k given a weight parameter λ (where $0 \leq \lambda \leq 1$) as:

$$r(w, k \mid \lambda) = \lambda \log(\phi_{kw}) + (1 - \lambda) \log\left(\frac{\phi_{kw}}{p_w}\right),$$

where λ determines the weight given to the probability of term w under topic k relative to its lift (measuring both on the log scale). Setting $\lambda = 1$ results in the familiar ranking of terms in decreasing order of their topic-specific probability, and setting $\lambda = 0$ ranks terms solely by their lift. We wish to learn an "optimal" value of λ for topic interpretation from our user study.

First, though, to see how different values of λ result in different ranked term lists, consider the plot in Figure 2. We fit a 50-topic model to the 20 Newsgroups data (details are described in Section 3.2) and plotted log(lift) on the y-axis vs. $\log(\phi_{kw})$ on the x-axis for each term in the vocabulary (which has size $V = 22,524$) for a given topic. Figure 2 shows this plot for Topic 29, which occurred mostly in documents posted to the "Motorcycles" Newsgroup, but also from documents posted to the "Automobiles" Newsgroup and the "Electronics" Newsgroup. Graphically, the line separating the most relevant terms for this topic, given λ, has slope $-\lambda/(1 - \lambda)$ (see Figure 2).

For this topic, the top-5 most relevant terms given $\lambda = 1$ (ranking solely by probability)

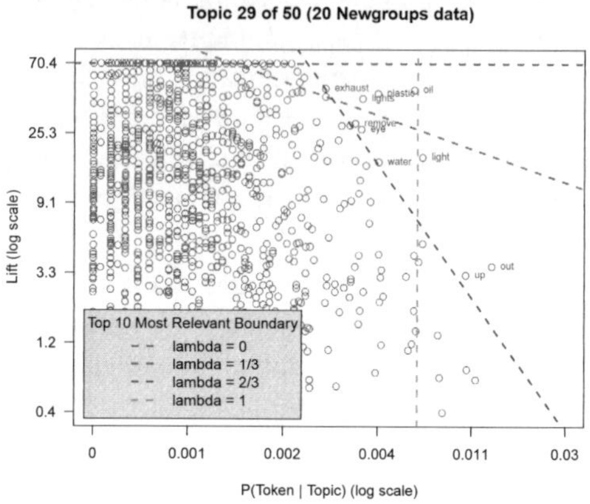

Figure 2: Dotted lines separating the top-10 most relevant terms for different values of λ, with the most relevant terms for $\lambda = 2/3$ displayed and highlighted in blue.

are {out, #emailaddress, #twodigitnumer, up, #onedigitnumber}, where a "#" symbol denotes a term that is an entity representing a class of things. In contrast to this list, which contains globally common terms and which provides very little meaning regarding motorcycles, automobiles, or electronics, the top-5 most relevant terms given $\lambda = 1/3$ are {oil, plastic, pipes, fluid, and lights}. The second set of terms is much more descriptive of the topic being discussed than the first.

3.2 User Study

We conducted a user study to determine whether there was an optimal value of λ in the definition of relevance to aid topic interpretation. First, we fit a 50-topic model to the $D = 13,695$ documents in the 20 Newsgroups data which were posted to a single Newsgroup (rather than two or more Newsgroups). We used the Collapsed Gibbs Sampler algorithm (Griffiths and Steyvers, 2004) to sample the latent topics for each of the $N = 1,590,376$ tokens in the data, and we saved their topic assignments from the last iteration (after convergence). We then computed the 20 by 50 table, T, which contains, in cell T_{gk}, the count of the number of times a token from topic $k \in \{1, ..., 50\}$ was assigned to Newsgroup $g \in \{1, ..., 20\}$, where we defined the Newsgroup of a token to be the Newsgroup to which the document containing that token was posted. Some of the LDA-inferred topics occurred almost exclusively ($> 90\%$ of occurrences) in documents from a single Newsgroup, such as Topic 38, which was the estimated topic for 15,705 tokens in the corpus, 14,233 of which came from documents posted to the "Medicine" (or "sci.med") Newsgroup. Other topics occurred in a wide variety of Newsgroups. One would expect these "spread-out" topics to be harder to interpret than the "pure" topics like Topic 38.

In the study we recruited 29 subjects among our colleagues (research scientists at AT&T Labs with moderate familiarity with text mining techniques and topic models), and each subject completed an online experiment consisting of 50 tasks, one for each topic in the fitted LDA model. Task k (for $k \in \{1, ..., 50\}$) was to read a list of five terms, ranked from 1-5 in order of relevance to topic k, where $\lambda \in (0, 1)$ was randomly sampled to compute relevance. The user was instructed to identify which "topic" the list of terms discussed from a list of three possible "topics", where their choices were names of the Newsgroups. The correct answer for task k (i.e. our "ground truth") was defined as the Newsgroup that contributed the most tokens to topic k (i.e. the Newsgroup with the largest count in the kth column of the table T), and the two alternative choices were the Newsgroups that contributed the second and third-most tokens to topic k.

We anticipated that the effect of λ on the probability of a user making the correct choice could be different across topics. In particular, for "spread-out" topics that were inherently difficult to interpret, because their tokens were drawn from a wide variety of Newsgroups (similar to a "fused" topic in Chuang et al. (2013b)), we expected the proportion of correct responses to be roughly 1/3 no matter the value of λ used to compute relevance. Similarly, for very "pure" topics, whose tokens were drawn almost exclusively from one Newsgroup, we expected the task to be easy for any value of λ. To account for this, we analyzed the experimental data by fitting a varying-intercepts logistic regression model to allow each of the fifty topics to have its own baseline difficulty level, where the effect of λ is shared across topics. We used a quadratic function of λ in the model (linear, cubic and quartic functions were explored and rejected).

As expected, the baseline difficulty of each topic varied widely. In fact, seven of the topics were correctly identified by all 29 users,[1] and one

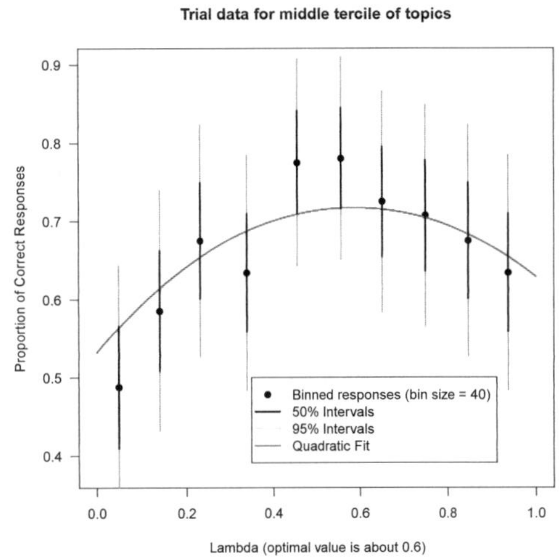

Figure 3: A plot of the proportion of correct responses in a user study vs. the value of λ used to compute the most relevant terms for each topic.

topic was incorrectly identified by all 29 users.[2] For the remaining 42 topics we estimated a topic-specific intercept term to control for the inherent difficulty of identifying the topic (not just due to its tokens being spread among multiple Newsgroups, but also to account for the inherent familiarity of each topic to our subject pool – subjects, on average, were more familiar with "Cars" than "The X Window System", for example).

The estimated effects of λ and λ^2 were 2.74 and -2.34, with standard errors 1.03 and 1.00. Taken together, their joint effect was statistically significant (χ^2 p-value = 0.018). To see the estimated effect of λ on the probability of correctly identifying a topic, consider Figure 3. We plot binned proportions of correct responses (on the y-axis) vs. λ (on the x-axis) for the 14 topics whose estimated topic-specific intercepts fell into the middle tercile among the 42 topics that weren't trivial or impossible to identify. Among these topics there was roughly a 67% baseline probability of correct identification. As Figure 3 shows, for these topics, the "optimal" value of λ was about 0.6, and it resulted in an estimated 70% probability of correct identification, whereas for values of λ near 0 and

[1]Whose ground truth labels were Medicine (twice), Miscellaneous Politics, Christianity, Gun Politics, Space (Astronomy), and Middle East Politics.

[2]The ground truth label for this topic was "Christianity", but the presence of the term "islam" or "quran" among the top-5 for every value of λ led each subject to choose "Miscellaneous Religion".

1, the estimated proportions of correct responses were closer to 53% and 63%, respectively. We view this as evidence that ranking terms according to relevance, where $\lambda < 1$ (i.e. not strictly in decreasing order of probability), can improve topic interpretability.

Note that in our experiment, we used the collection of single-posted 20 Newsgroups documents to define our "ground truth" data. An alternative method for collecting "ground truth" data would have been to recruit experts to label topics from an LDA model. We chose against this option because doing so would present a classic "chicken-or-egg" problem: If we use expert-labeled topics in an experiment to learn how to summarize topics so that they can be interpreted (i.e. "labeled"), we would only re-learn the way that our experts were instructed, or allowed, to label the topics in the first place! If, for instance, the experts were presented with a ranked list of the most probable terms for each topic, this would influence the interpretations and labels they give to the topics, and the experimental result would be the circular conclusion that ranking terms by probability allows users to recover the "expert" labels most easily. To avoid this, we felt strongly that we should use data in which documents have metadata associated with them. The 20 Newsgroups data provides an externally validated source of topic labels, in the sense that the labels were presented to users (in the form of Newsgroup names), and users subsequently filled in the content. It represents, essentially, a crowd-sourced collection of tokens, or content, for a certain set of topic labels.

4 The `LDAvis` System

Our interactive, web-based visualization system, `LDAvis`, has two core functionalities that enable users to understand the topic-term relationships in a fitted LDA model, and a number of extra features that provide additional perspectives on the model.

First and foremost, `LDAvis` allows one to select a topic to reveal the most relevant terms for that topic. In Figure 1, Topic 34 is selected, and its 30 most relevant terms (given $\lambda = 0.34$, in this case) populate the barchart to the right (ranked in order of relevance from top to bottom). The widths of the gray bars represent the corpus-wide frequencies of each term, and the widths of the red bars represent the topic-specific frequencies of each term. A slider allows users to change the value of λ, which can alter the rankings of terms to aid topic interpretation. By default, λ is set to 0.6, as suggested by our user study in Section 3.2. If $\lambda = 1$, terms are ranked solely by ϕ_{kw}, which implies the red bars would be sorted from widest (at the top) to narrowest (at the bottom). By comparing the widths of the red and gray bars for a given term, users can quickly understand whether a term is highly relevant to the selected topic because of its lift (a high ratio of red to gray), or its probability (absolute width of red). The top 3 most relevant terms in Figure 1 are "law", "court", and "cruel". Note that "law" is a common term which is generated by Topic 34 in about 40% of its corpus-wide occurrences, whereas "cruel" is a relatively rare term with very high lift in Topic 34 – it occurs almost exclusively in this topic. Such properties of the topic-term relationships are readily visible in `LDAvis` for every topic.

On the left panel, two visual features provide a global perspective of the topics. First, the areas of the circles are proportional to the relative prevalences of the topics in the corpus. In the 50-topic model fit to the 20 Newsgroups data, the first three topics comprise 12%, 9%, and 6% of the corpus, and all contain common, non-specific terms (although there are interesting differences: Topic 2 contains formal debate-related language such as "conclusion", "evidence", and "argument", whereas Topic 3 contains slang conversational language such as "kinda", "like", and "yeah"). In addition to visualizing topic prevalence, the left pane shows inter-topic differences. The default for computing inter-topic distances is Jensen-Shannon divergence, although other metrics are enabled. The default for scaling the set of inter-topic distances defaults to Principal Components, but other algorithms are also enabled.

The second core feature of `LDAvis` is the ability to select a term (by hovering over it) to reveal its conditional distribution over topics. This distribution is visualized by altering the areas of the topic circles such that they are proportional to the term-specific frequencies across the corpus. This allows the user to verify, as discussed in Chuang et al. (2012a), whether the multidimensional scaling of topics has faithfully clustered similar topics in two-dimensional space. For example, in Figure 4, the term "file" is selected. In the majority of this term's occurrences, it is drawn from one of several topics located in the upper left-hand region of the

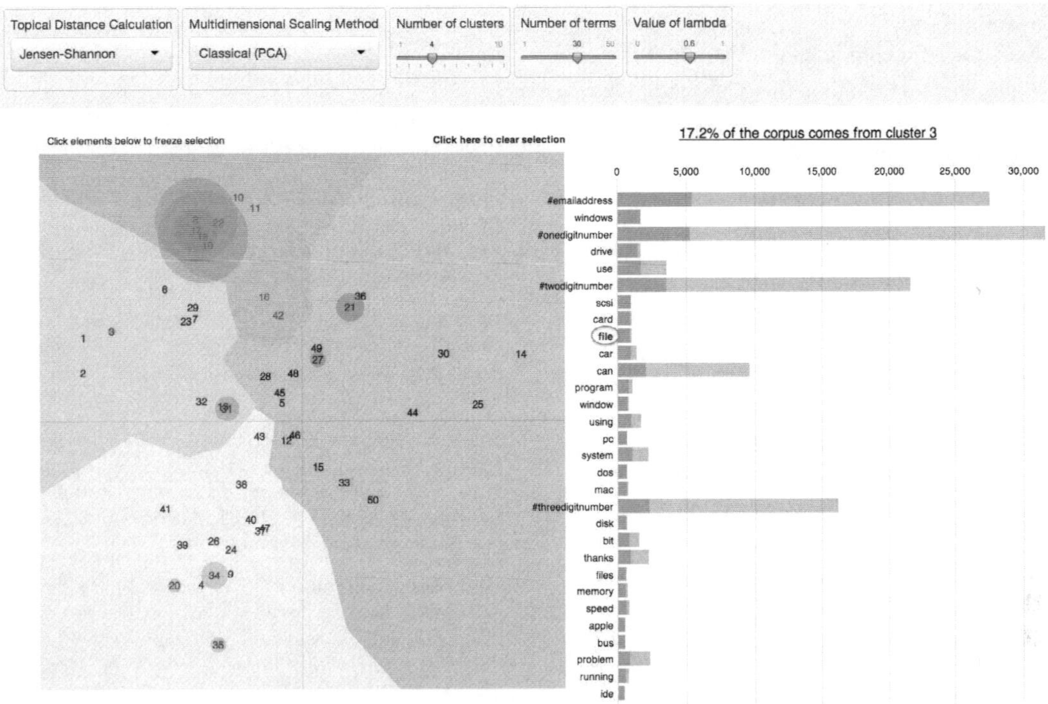

Figure 4: The user has chosen to segment the fifty topics into four clusters, and has selected the green cluster to populate the barchart with the most relevant terms for that cluster. Then, the user hovered over the ninth bar from the top, "file", to display the conditional distribution over topics for this term.

global topic view. Upon inspection, this group of topics can be interpreted broadly as a discussion of computer hardware and software. This verifies, to some extent, their placement, via multidimensional scaling, into the same two-dimensional region. It also suggests that the term "file" used in this context refers to a computer file. However, there is also conditional probability mass for the term "file" on Topic 34. As shown in Figure 1, Topic 34 can be interpreted as discussing the criminal punishment system where "file" refers to court filings. Similar discoveries can be made for any term that exhibits polysemy (such as "drive" appearing in computer- and automobile-related topics, for example).

Beyond its within-browser interaction capability using D3 (Bostock et al., 2011), `LDAvis` leverages the `R` language (R Core Team, 2014) and specifically, the `shiny` package (Rstudio, 2014), to allow users to easily alter the topical distance measurement as well as the multidimensional scaling algorithm to produce the global topic view. In addition, there is an option to apply k-means clustering to the topics (as a function of their two-dimensional locations in the global topic view). This is merely an effort to facilitate semantic zooming in an LDA model with many topics where 'after-the-fact' clustering may be an easier way to estimate clusters of topics, rather than fitting a hierarchical topic model (Blei et al., 2003), for example. Selecting a cluster of topics (by clicking the Voronoi region corresponding to the cluster) reveals the most relevant terms for that cluster of topics, where the term distribution of a cluster of topics is defined as the weighted average of the term distributions of the individual topics in the cluster. In Figure 4, the green cluster of topics is selected, and the most relevant terms, displayed in the barchart on the right, are predominantly related to computer hardware and software.

5 Discussion

We have described a web-based, interactive visualization system, `LDAvis`, that enables deep inspection of topic-term relationships in an LDA model, while simultaneously providing a global view of the topics, via their prevalences and similarities to each other, in a compact space. We also propose a novel measure, *relevance*, by which to rank terms within topics to aid in the task of topic interpretation, and we present results from a user study that show that ranking terms in decreasing order of probability is suboptimal for topic interpretation. The `LDAvis` visualization system (including the user study data) is currently available as an `R` package on GitHub: https://github.com/cpsievert/LDAvis.

For future work, we anticipate performing a larger user study to further understand how to facilitate topic interpretation in fitted LDA models, including a comparison of multiple methods, such as ranking by Turbo Topics (Blei and Lafferty, 2009) or FREX scores (Bischof and Airoldi, 2012), in addition to relevance. We also note the need to visualize correlations between topics, as this can provide insight into what is happening on the document level without actually displaying entire documents. Last, we seek a solution to the problem of visualizing a large number of topics (say, from 100 - 500 topics) in a compact way.

References

Loulwah AlSumait, Daniel Barbara, James Gentle, and Carlotta Domeniconi. 2009. *Topic Significance Ranking of LDA Generative Models*. ECML.

Jonathan M. Bischof and Edoardo M. Airoldi. 2012. *Summarizing topical content with word frequency and exclusivity*. ICML.

David M. Blei, Andrew Y. Ng, and Michael I. Jordan. 2012. *Latent Dirichlet Allocation*. JMLR.

David M. Blei and John Lafferty. 2009. Visualizing Topics with Multi-Word Expressions. arXiv:0907.1013v1 [stat.ML], 2009

David M. Blei, Thomas L. Griffiths, Michael I. Jordan, and Joshua B. Tenenbaum. 2003. *Hierarchical Topic Models and the Nested Chinese Restaurant Process*. NIPS.

Michael Bostock, Vadim Ogievetsky, Jeffrey Heer 2011. *D3: Data-Driven Documents*. InfoVis.

Allison J.B. Chaney and David M. Blei. 2012. *Visualizing topic models*. ICWSM.

Jonathan Chang, Jordan Boyd-Graber, Sean Gerrish, Chong Wang, and David M. Blei. 2009. *Reading Tea Leaves: How Humans Interpret Topic Models*. NIPS.

Jason Chuang, Daniel Ramage, Christopher D. Manning and Jeffrey Heer. 2012a. *Interpretation and Trust: Designing Model-Driven Visualizations for Text Analysis*. CHI.

Jason Chuang, Christopher D. Manning and Jeffrey Heer. 2012b. *Termite: Visualization Techniques for Assessing Textual Topic Models*. AVI.

Jason Chuang, Yuening Hu, Ashley Jin, John D. Wilkerson, Daniel A. McFarland, Christopher D. Manning and Jeffrey Heer. 2013a. *Document Exploration with Topic Modeling: Designing Interactive Visualizations to Support Effective Analysis Workflows*. NIPS Workshop on Topic Models: Computation, Application, and Evaluation.

Jason Chuang, Sonal Gupta, Christopher D. Manning and Jeffrey Heer. 2013b. *Topic Model Diagnostics: Assessing Domain Relevance via Topical Alignment*. ICML.

Matthew J. Gardner, Joshua Lutes, Jeff Lund, Josh Hansen, Dan Walker, Eric Ringger, and Kevin Seppi. 2010. *The topic browser: An interactive tool for browsing topic models*. NIPS Workshop on Challenges of Data Visualization.

Brynjar Gretarsson, John O'Donovan, Svetlin Bostandjieb, Tobias Hollerer, Arthur Asuncion, David Newman, and Padhraic Smyth. 2011. *TopicNets: Visual Analysis of Large Text Corpora with Topic Modeling*. ACM Transactions on Intelligent Systems and Technology, pp 1-26.

Thomas L. Griffiths and Mark Steyvers. 2004. *Finding scientific topics*. PNAS.

David Mimno, Hanna M. Wallach, Edmund Talley, Miriam Leenders, and Andrew McCallum. 2011. *Optimizing Semantic Coherence in Topic Models*. EMNLP.

David Newman, Youn Noh, Edmund Talley, Sarvnaz Karimi, and Timothy Baldwin 2010. *Evaluating Topic Models for Digital Libraries*. JCDL.

R Core Team 2014. *R: A Language and Environment for Statistical Computing*. http://www.R-project.org.

R Studio, Inc. 2014. *shiny: Web Application Framework for R; package version 0.9.1*. http://CRAN.R-project.org/package=shiny.

Daniel Ramage, Evan Rosen and Jason Chuang and Christopher D. Manning, and Daniel A. McFarland. 2009. *Topic Modeling for the Social Sciences*. NIPS Workshop on Applications for Topic Models: Text and Beyond.

Justin Snyder, Rebecca Knowles, Mark Dredze, Matthew Gormley, and Travis Wolfe. 2013. *Topic Models and Metadata for Visualizing Text Corpora*. Proceedings of the 2013 NAACL HLT Demonstration Session.

Matthew A. Taddy 2011. *On Estimation and Selection for Topic Models*. AISTATS.

Hanna M. Wallach, Iain Murray, Ruslan Salakhutdinov, and David Mimno. 2009. *Evaluation Methods for Topic Models*. ICML.

Hiérarchie: Interactive Visualization for Hierarchical Topic Models

Alison Smith, Timothy Hawes, and Meredith Myers
DECISIVE ANALYTICS Corporation
Arlington, VA
{alison.smith, timothy.hawes, meredith.myers}@dac.us

Abstract

Existing algorithms for understanding large collections of documents often produce output that is nearly as difficult and time consuming to interpret as reading each of the documents themselves. Topic modeling is a text understanding algorithm that discovers the "topics" or themes within a collection of documents. Tools based on topic modeling become increasingly complex as the number of topics required to best represent the collection increases. In this work, we present Hiérarchie, an interactive visualization that adds structure to large topic models, making them approachable and useful to an end user. Additionally, we demonstrate Hiérarchie's ability to analyze a diverse document set regarding a trending news topic.

1 Introduction

In computational linguistics and related fields, significant work has been invested in the development of algorithms for gaining insight from large bodies of text. The raw output of these techniques can be so complex that it is just as difficult and time consuming to understand as reading the text. Therefore, it is an especially challenging problem to develop visualizations that add *analytic value*, making complex analysis accessible by helping a user to understand and interact with the output of these algorithms.

Topic Modeling is a common, data-driven technique for summarizing the content of large text corpora. This technique models documents as distributions of topics and topics as distributions of words. In practice, topic models are used to provide a high-level overview and guided exploration of a corpus. Prior work by others (Chaney and Blei, 2012) and by the author (Smith et al., 2014) has focused on visualizing the results of topic modeling to support these two goals, but these visualizations do not scale beyond 10 to 20 topics[1]. Topic models with a small number of topics may not accurately represent very diverse corpora; instead, representative topic models require a number of topics an order of magnitude higher, for which current visualization methods are not suitable. We propose a visualization that displays hierarchically arranged topics. As opposed to a flat model, which can be thought of as an unordered heap of topics, a hierarchical structure allows a user to "drill into" topics of interest, meaning this technique supports directed exploration of a corpus regardless of the number of topics in the model.

Although methods that use inherently hierarchical generative models do exist, we take a simple recursive approach that scales to large datasets and does not change or depend on the underlying topic modeling implementation. In principle, this technique could be applied to a range of topic modeling algorithms. We present this hierarchical model to the user through an intuitive interactive visualization, Hiérarchie. Additionally, we demonstrate the capability with a Case Study on analyzing the news coverage surrounding the Malaysia Airlines flight that went missing on March 8, 2014.

2 Related Work

Latent Dirichlet Allocation (LDA) (Blei et al., 2003b) is an unsupervised algorithm for performing statistical topic modeling that uses a "bag of words" approach, treating each document as a set of unordered words. Each document is represented as a probability distribution over some topics, and each topic is a probability distribution over

[1]Either the visualization becomes too confusing to understand or using the visualization to explore the corpus takes too much time — or both.

Proceedings of the Workshop on Interactive Language Learning, Visualization, and Interfaces, pages 71–78,
Baltimore, Maryland, USA, June 27, 2014. ©2014 Association for Computational Linguistics

words. LDA is an effective, scalable approach to modeling a large text corpus; however, the result is a flat topic model with no hierarchical structure for a visualization to exploit.

Approaches exist for learning topic hierarchies from data, such as the Nested Chinese restaurant process (Blei et al., 2003a) and Pachinko Allocation (Li and McCallum, 2006). These approaches build the intuitions of the hierarchy into the modeling algorithm. This adds additional complexity and tightly couples the hierarchical process with the underlying modeling algorithm.

Our Hierarchical Topic Modeling method uses a simple top-down recursive approach of splitting and re-modeling a corpus to produce a hierarchical topic model that does not require a specific underlying topic modeling algorithm. This work is most similar to Dirichlet Compound Multinomial Latent Dirichlet Allocation, DCM-LDA, which processes the corpus via a bottom-up approach. DCM-LDA first trains unique topic models based on co-occurrence of words in each document, and then clusters topics across documents (Mimno and McCallum, 2007).

Existing visualizations support analysis and exploration of topic models. Topical Guide (Gardner et al., 2010), TopicViz (Eisenstein et al., 2012), and the topic visualization of (Chaney and Blei, 2012) provide visualization and interaction with topic models for corpus exploration and understanding. These visualizations typically represent topics as word clouds, where the topic model as a whole is presented as an unordered set of topics. This approach is not optimal for efficient exploration and understanding, and the *sea of word clouds* quickly becomes overwhelming as the number of topics grows. Termite (Chuang et al., 2012) uses a tabular layout to represent a topic model and supports easy comparison of words within and across topics. The Termite visualization organizes the model into clusters of *related* topics based on word overlap. This visualization technique is space saving and the clustering speeds corpus understanding. Our approach clusters topics by document overlap instead of word overlap and is hierarchical, providing multiple levels of related topics for intuitive corpus exploration.

Nested lists, icicle plots (Kruskal and Landwehr, 1983), and treemaps (Shneiderman, 1998) are commonly used for visualizing hierarchical data, but they have limitations and do not easily support data-dense hierarchies, such as hierarchical topic models. Nested lists can be hard to navigate as they fail to maintain the same size and approximate structure during exploration. An icicle plot, which is a vertical representation of a partition chart, suffers from similar rendering constraints and limits positioning, sizing, and readability of text labeling. Treemaps use nested rectangles to display hierarchical data, but have been criticized as not *cognitively plausible* (Fabrikant and Skupin, 2005), making them difficult to interpret. Additionally, as is the case for nested lists and icicle plots, treemaps obscure the structure of the underlying data to accommodate layout and sizing constraints.

Hiérarchie uses an interactive sunburst chart (Stasko et al., 2000), which is a partition chart with radial orientation that supports visualizing large or small hierarchies without requiring scrolling or other interaction. The sunburst chart implementation used by Hiérarchie is directly based upon the Sequences Sunburst (Rodden, 2013) and Zoomable Sunburst (Bostock, 2012b) examples that are implemented in the Data-Driven Documents library (Bostock, 2012a).

3 Hierarchical Topic Modeling

The HLDA algorithm takes a simple, top-down approach for producing hierarchical topic models by recursively splitting and re-modeling a corpus. Standard LDA discovers the distribution of words in topics and topics in documents through an inference process; our implementation uses Gibbs sampling (Griffiths and Steyvers, 2004) for inference. As a result of this process, each word in a document is assigned to a topic. At the end of sampling, HLDA uses these word-to-topic assignments to construct new *synthetic* documents for each topic from each of the initial documents. These synthetic documents contain only those words from the original document that are assigned to the topic and make up the synthetic corpus for the topic. So, if there are 10 topics in the topic model, up to 10 new synthetic documents — one for each topic — will be created for each document, and these documents will be merged into the topic's synthetic corpus.

For each topic, t, we then construct a new topic model, m_t, using the synthetic corpus corresponding to t. The discovered topics in m_t represent the *subtopics* of t. This process, illustrated in

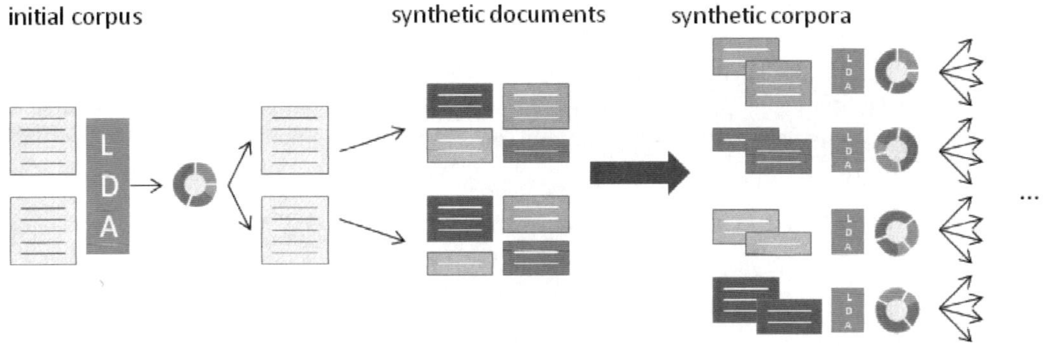

Figure 1: Overview of the HLDA algorithm. The algorithm runs LDA over the original corpus which results in a topic model and word-topic assignments. These word-topic assignments are used to create synthetic documents — one for each document/topic pair. The synthetic documents are grouped into synthetic corpora by topic, and LDA is run for each of the synthetic corpora. This process continues recursively until the synthetic corpus and documents are too small to model. The result is a hierarchy of topic distributions.

Figure 1, can be repeated recursively, until the synthetic corpus and synthetic documents are too small to model.[2] While the number of topics at each level in the hierarchy must be specified, the overall number of topics discovered by this approach is a byproduct of the algorithm.

This modeling approach is a wrapper algorithm that can be applied to any modeling approach that assigns individual tokens in documents to specific topics.

4 Hiérarchie

To effectively visualize the topic hierarchy output from HLDA, it is important to properly convey the relevance and structure of the topics. Intuitive interaction with the visualization is important so users can easily explore topics and identify patterns. Without effective visualization, forming conclusions becomes as difficult as approaching the raw documents without the benefit of algorithmic analysis.

In practice, a diverse set of visualizations are used to display hierarchical data. An effective visualization of a hierarchical topic model should support the following Use Cases:

1. **Accuracy** - display topics without hiding or skewing the hierarchical structure
2. **Granularity** - interact with the visualization to explore the topics at all levels of the hierarchy
3. **Accessibility** - view the underlying data associated with the topics

[2]This is parameterized and can be set based on tolerable quality degradation from short documents or small corpora.

Many of the visualizations we considered for viewing topic hierarchies obscure or misrepresent the true structure of their underlying data, largely due to the amount of space required for rendering. Others provide less skewing of the structure, yet, for large hierarchies, require a high degree of user interaction (clicking and navigating) to expose the underlying data. We found that a sunburst chart is best suited to our purposes as it supports visualizing large or small hierarchies without requiring scrolling or other interaction. Unlike other hierarchical visualizations, the sunburst can accommodate the size of a typical computer screen without hiding or minimizing structure.

Figure 2 displays a top-level view of the Hiérarchie visualization for a dataset of Tweets, Reddit comments, and news articles regarding the Malaysia Airlines flight. Each level of the hierarchical topic model is represented as a ring of the Sunburst chart where the arcs comprising the rings represent the individual topics. By not labeling each arc, or "slice," within the sunburst, the high-level overview of the hierarchical topic model is presented to the user with minimal complexity.

The initial, high-level view of the sunburst chart follows the design principle of *overview first, zoom and filter, details on demand* (Shnei-

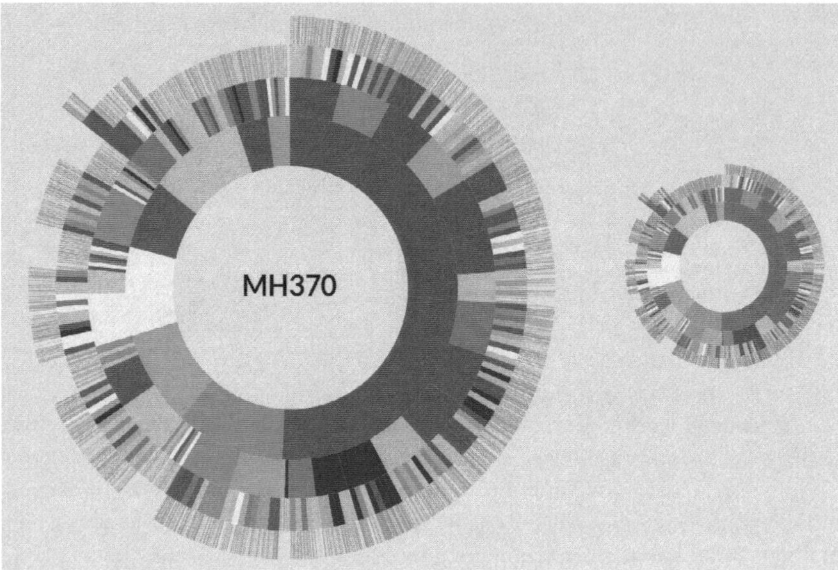

Figure 2: The top-level view of the Hiérarchie visualization. This visualization uses a sunburst chart, which is optimal for displaying the topic hierarchy created by the HLDA algorithm without hiding or skewing the hierarchical structure.

derman, 1996) and does not display details for every topic, requiring user interaction to expose additional data. In our sunburst visualization, user interaction allows for exploration of the information at a finer granularity. When hovering over a topic of interest, the words of the topic are displayed in the empty center of the sunburst. This is an efficient use of space and prevents disorientation, since minimal eye movement is required between the slice of interest (where the user's mouse is located) and the center list of topics.

When a user selects a slice of interest, the sunburst zooms in to display the selected topic and sub-topics. This allows the user to analyze a specific section of the hierarchy. This interaction is shown in Figures 4 and 5. The sunburst has reoriented to display the selected sub-topic, (plane, crash, crashed) as the visualization root.

To provide a clean and meaningful display of topic information for each slice, only one slice's information can be shown at a time. As the sunburst zooms to display selected topics, it is useful to provide context for the location of the topic within the overall topic hierarchy. Therefore, two contextual visualizations — a breadcrumb trail and a contextual anchor — are provided. Breadcrumb trails are often utilized to provide context during navigation, such as when navigating a file structure or large retail website. The breadcrumb trail displays the hierarchical path leading to the current topic (Aery, 2007). A contextual anchor, or *contextual snapshot* (Mindek et al., 2013), is used to provide additional context to the user. The contextual anchor displays the entire hierarchical topic model to the user at all times. When the user selects a topic slice to view a section of the hierarchy in more detail, the contextual anchor highlights the position of the selected topic within the hierarchical topic model. This offers context to the user, regardless of their location within the hierarchy. An example of the breadcrumb trail and contextual anchor is displayed in Figure 3.

5 Case Study

The search for Malaysia Flight MH-370 was ongoing during the composition of this paper, with few clues indicating what might have actually occurred. In an attempt to organize the various theories, we collected 1600 Tweets and 970 Reddit comments containing the keyword "MH370" in addition to 27 Daily Beast articles returned by a URL filter for any of the key words "malay," "370", "flight," "missing," "hijack," "radar," "pilot," "plane," "airplane," and "wreckage." This corpus offers a diverse sampling of discussion concerning the missing airliner that is too large for a human alone to quickly analyze. We pro-

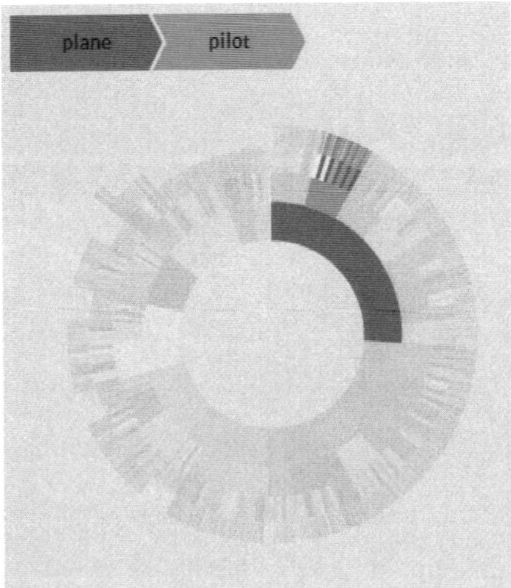

Figure 3: Our simple breadcrumb trail and contextual anchor offer constant context as the user explores the visualization. Highlighted slices within the contextual anchor are those currently displayed in the sunburst visualization.

cessed the corpus with HLDA using 10 topics for each level. This number of topics balances granularity and accuracy. Using too many narrow topics results in information overload, whereas too few broad topics could be difficult to understand[3]. We then visualized the resulting hierarchical topic model with Hiérarchie as shown in Figure 2. As we were most interested in looking at the various theories surrounding the flight, we chose to explore one of the high-level topics, (plane, people, pilot, think, know), in more detail, because many of this topic's sub-topics suggest specific theories related to the outcome of MH-370. Table 1 shows the 10 sub-topics for the "theory" topic represented by their 3 most probable terms. The bolded topics are those that suggest theories. Figure 4 shows the sunburst graph reoriented after the selection of the main "theory" topic. The sunburst graph is labeled with the sub-topics that represent the selection of interesting theories.

These topics suggest four primary theories: that the plane landed, the plane crashed, the plane was hijacked by terrorists, or the pilot crashed the plane in an act of suicide. Hovering over the (*plane, crash, crashed*) topic shows the sub topics, and clicking the topic reorients the sunburst chart,

[3]Deviating from this number slightly may also be effective, and experimentation is required to determine the number of topics that is the best fit for the current data set and end goal.

plane, crash, crashed
plane, landed, land
plane, think, people
pilot, plane, hijacking
terrorist, terrorism, passports
suicide, pilot, ocean
Shah, Anwar, political
plane, China, world
phone, phones, cell
evidence, think, make

Table 1: The 10 high-level topics of the model generated from running HLDA on the Malaysia Flight MH-370 corpus. The bolded topics suggest specific theories regarding the status of the plane.

crash, water, crashed
failure, catastrophic, mayday
mechanical, failure, days
plane, ocean, did
plane, error, lost

Table 2: A selection of the sub-topics of discussion surrounding a plane crash scenario. These sub-topics suggest more detailed discussion. For example, that the plane crash may have resulted from a catastrophic mechanical failure or other error.

as shown in Figure 5. The sub-topics under (*plane, crash, crashed*) suggest more detailed discussion of a crash scenario, such as the plane crashing into the water, and that there may have been a catastrophic mechanical failure or other error. Table 2 contains a selection of these sub-topics.

An alternate theory is suggested by the (*terrorist, terrorism, passports*) topic, which is shown in Figure 6. The sub-topics here suggest more detailed discussion involving terrorism as the cause for the plane's disappearance. Table 3 contains a selection of these sub-topics.

The hierarchical topic model produced by HLDA and visualized with Hiéarchie provide automated organization of the many theories regarding the missing Malaysian airliner. The high-level overview provides a quick summary of all of the discussion surrounding the event, while the hierarchical organization and intuitive exploration allows the discussion, and specifically each theory, to be explored in depth, exposing potentially

passports, stolen, using
terrorists, crash, terrorist
Muslim, Muslims, Islamic
attack, going, terror
responsibility, common, group

Table 3: A selection of the sub-topics of discussion surrounding a terrorism scenario. These subtopics include more details, such as the discussion of stolen passports, relevant to the theory that the plane disappearance is the result of an act of terrorism.

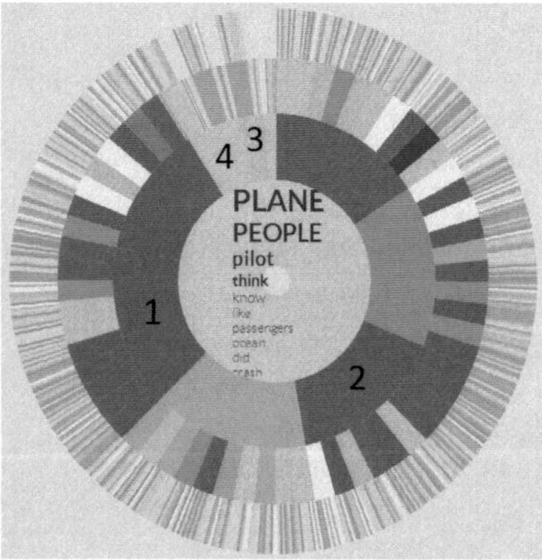

Figure 4: Sub-categories of interest have been purposely numbered for clarity. 1:(*plane*, *crash*, *crashed*); 2: (*plane*, *landed*, *land*); 3: (*terrorist*, *terrorism*, *passports*); 4: (*suicide*, *pilot*, *ocean*).

relevant information. Organizing all of this data by hand would be difficult and time consuming. This intuitive visualization in combination with our method for organizing the underlying data transforms a disparate corpus of documents into a useful and manageable information source.

6 Future Work and Conclusion

The Hiéarchie visualization and related hierarchical topic modeling algorithm support the understanding and exploration of text corpora that are too large to read. Although existing topic modeling algorithms effectively process large corpora, the resulting topic models are difficult to interpret in their raw format. Current visualization methods only scale to a small number of topics, which cannot accurately represent a diverse corpus. Additional structure is required to organize a representative topic model of a large dataset into an un-

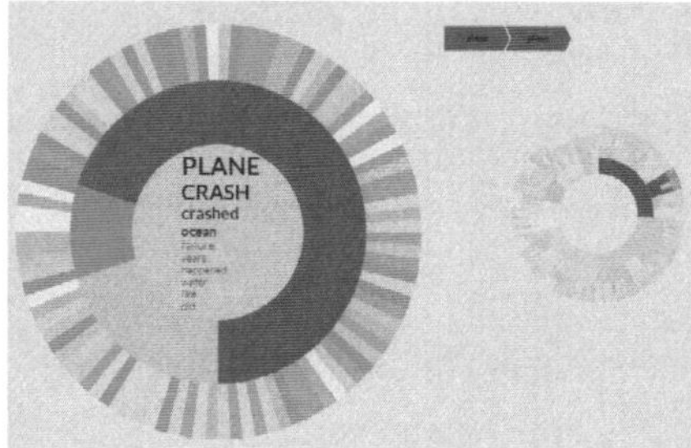

Figure 5: Clicking the (*plane*, *crash*, *crashed*) topic slice in the top-level (*plane*, *people*, *pilot*) visualization reorients the sunburst to display the slice as its root, enabling more detailed exploration of sub-topics.

Figure 6: The(*terrorist*, *terrorism*, *passports*) topic slice in the top-level (*plane*, *people*, *pilot*) visualization.

derstandable and navigable analysis tool.

Our approach visualizes the hierarchical topic model produced by the HLDA algorithm to support intuitive, directed browsing of topical structure within a diverse collection of documents. As demonstrated in the Malaysia Airlines case study, this technique can be used to quickly gain insight about the diverse speculation surrounding a significant, inconclusive event. Hiéarchie enables users to examine and gain insight from large, diverse datasets more efficiently than if they had to interpret complicated algorithmic output or read raw documents.

The sunburst visualization provides a clear overview of the structure of the model; however, individual topics are currently represented as lists of words ordered by their probability for the topic. This is non-optimal for topic understanding. Additionally, this topic information is displayed on hover, which does not easily support making comparisons between topics. Future work includes implementing alternative techniques for displaying the topic information and performing an evaluation to determine which technique is most appropriate for the intended use cases.

Future work also includes adding additional information to the visualization through color and topic placement. In the current implementation, topic slices are currently colored by the most prevalent topic word. Coloring slices by sentiment or other topic-level metrics will enrich the visualization and improve the user's ability to quickly discern different topics and their meaning within the model as a whole. Similarly, topic position in the sunburst does not currently provide any useful information. One possible layout is based on topic covariance, which is a metric of topic relatedness based on the frequency of topic pair co-occurrence within the documents of the corpus. An improved sunburst layout could take into account topic covariance to optimize the layout such that related topics were positioned together at each level of the hierarchy.

Acknowledgements

We would like to thank Andrew McCallum for discussions related to the ideas behind our topic modeling approach. We would also like to thank Mark Frymire, Peter David, Jen Sikos, and Nichole Hansen for their support in the writing process. Additionally, we would like to acknowledge that this work was performed under AFRL contract FA8750-12-C-0077. The opinions and conclusions do not reflect the position of the Air Force.

References

Sean C Aery. 2007. Breadcrumb navigation deployment patterns in retail web sites.

David M Blei, Thomas L Griffiths, Michael I Jordan, and Joshua B Tenenbaum. 2003a. Hierarchical topic models and the nested chinese restaurant process. In *NIPS*, volume 16.

David M Blei, Andrew Y Ng, and Michael I Jordan. 2003b. Latent dirichlet allocation. *the Journal of machine Learning research*, 3:993–1022.

Mike Bostock. 2012a. Data Driven Documents (d3). http://d3js.org.

Mike Bostock. 2012b. Zoomable sunburst. http://bl.ocks.org/mbostock/4348373.

Allison June-Barlow Chaney and David M Blei. 2012. Visualizing topic models. In *ICWSM*.

Jason Chuang, Christopher D Manning, and Jeffrey Heer. 2012. Termite: Visualization techniques for assessing textual topic models. In *Proceedings of the International Working Conference on Advanced Visual Interfaces*, pages 74–77. ACM.

Jacob Eisenstein, Duen Horng Chau, Aniket Kittur, and Eric Xing. 2012. Topicviz: interactive topic exploration in document collections. In *CHI'12 Extended Abstracts*, pages 2177–2182. ACM.

Sara Irina Fabrikant and André Skupin. 2005. Cognitively plausible information visualization.

Matthew J Gardner, Joshua Lutes, Jeff Lund, Josh Hansen, Dan Walker, Eric Ringger, and Kevin Seppi. 2010. The topic browser: An interactive tool for browsing topic models. In *NIPS Workshop on Challenges of Data Visualization*.

Thomas L Griffiths and Mark Steyvers. 2004. Finding scientific topics. *Proceedings of the National academy of Sciences of the United States of America*, 101(Suppl 1):5228–5235.

Joseph B Kruskal and James M Landwehr. 1983. Icicle plots: Better displays for hierarchical clustering. *The American Statistician*, 37(2):162–168.

Wei Li and Andrew McCallum. 2006. Pachinko allocation: Dag-structured mixture models of topic correlations.

David Mimno and Andrew McCallum. 2007. Organizing the oca: learning faceted subjects from a library of digital books. In *Proceedings of the 7th ACM/IEEE-CS joint conference on Digital libraries*, pages 376–385. ACM.

Peter Mindek, Stefan Bruckner, and M Eduard Gröller. 2013. Contextual snapshots: Enriched visualization with interactive spatial annotations. In *Proceedings of the 29th Spring conference on Computer Graphics (SCCG 2013)*.

Kerry Rodden. 2013. Sequences sunburst. http://bl.ocks.org/kerryrodden/7090426.

Ben Shneiderman. 1996. The eyes have it: A task by data type taxonomy for information visualizations. In *Visual Languages, 1996. Proceedings., IEEE Symposium on*, pages 336–343. IEEE.

Ben Shneiderman. 1998. Treemaps for space-constrained visualization of hierarchies.

Alison Smith, Sana Malik, and Ben Shneiderman. 2014. Visual analysis of topical evolution in unstructured text: Design and evaluation of topicflow.

John Stasko, Richard Catrambone, Mark Guzdial, and Kevin McDonald. 2000. An evaluation of space-filling information visualizations for depicting hierarchical structures. *International Journal of Human-Computer Studies*, 53(5):663–694.

Concurrent Visualization of Relationships between Words and Topics in Topic Models

Alison Smith*, **Jason Chuang**†, **Yuening Hu***, **Jordan Boyd-Graber***, **Leah Findlater***
*University of Maryland, College Park, MD
†University of Washington, Seattle, WA
amsmit@cs.umd.edu, jcchuang@cs.washington.edu, ynhu@cs.umd.edu, jbg@umiacs.umd.edu, leahkf@umd.edu

Abstract

Analysis tools based on topic models are often used as a means to explore large amounts of unstructured data. Users often reason about the correctness of a model using relationships between words within the topics or topics within the model. We compute this useful contextual information as term co-occurrence and topic covariance and overlay it on top of standard topic model output via an intuitive interactive visualization. This is a work in progress with the end goal to combine the visual representation with interactions and online learning, so the users can directly explore (a) why a model may not align with their intuition and (b) modify the model as needed.

1 Introduction

Topic modeling is a popular technique for analyzing large text corpora. A user is unlikely to have the time required to understand and exploit the raw results of topic modeling for analysis of a corpus. Therefore, an interesting and intuitive visualization is required for a topic model to provide added value. A common topic modeling technique is Latent Dirichlet Allocation (LDA) (Blei et al., 2003), which is an unsupervised algorithm for performing statistical topic modeling that uses a "bag of words" approach. The resulting topic model represents the corpus as an unrelated set of topics where each topic is a probability distribution over words. Experienced users who have worked with a text corpus for an extended period of time often think of the thematic relationships in the corpus in terms of higher-level statistics such as (a) inter-topic correlations or (b) word correlations. However, standard topic models do not explicitly provide such contextual information to the users.

Existing tools based on topic models, such as Topical Guide (Gardner et al., 2010), TopicViz (Eisenstein et al., 2012), and the topic visualization of (Chaney and Blei, 2012) support topic-based corpus browsing and understanding. Visualizations of this type typically represent standard topic models as a *sea of word clouds*; the individual topics within the model are presented as an unordered set of word clouds — or something similar — of the top words for the topic[1] where word size is proportional to the probability of the word for the topic. A primary issue with word clouds is that they can hinder understanding (Harris, 2011) due to the fact that they lack information about the relationships between words. Additionally, topic model visualizations that display topics in a random layout can lead to a huge, inefficiently organized search space, which is not always helpful in providing a quick corpus overview or assisting the user to diagnose possible problems with the model.

The authors of Correlated Topic Models (CTM) (Lafferty and Blei, 2006) recognize the limitation of existing topic models to directly model the correlation between topics, and present an alternative algorithm, CTM, which models the correlation between topics discovered for a corpus by using a more flexible distribution for the topic proportions in the model. Topical n-gram models (TNG) (Wang et al., 2007) discover phrases in addition to topics. TNG is a probabilistic model which assigns words and n-grams based on surrounding context, instead of for all references in the corpus. These models independently account for the two limitations of statistical topic modeling discussed in this paper by modifying the underlying topic modeling algorithm. Our work aims to provide a low-cost method for incorporating this

[1]This varies, but typically is either the top 10 to 20 words or the number of words which hold a specific portion of the distribution weight.

Proceedings of the Workshop on Interactive Language Learning, Visualization, and Interfaces, pages 79–82,
Baltimore, Maryland, USA, June 27, 2014. ©2014 Association for Computational Linguistics

information as well as visualizing it in an effective way. We compute summary statistics, term co-occurrence and topic covariance, which can be overlaid on top of any traditional topic model. As a number of application-specific LDA implementations exist, we propose a meta-technique which can be applied to any underlying algorithm.

We present a *relationship-enriched* visualization to help users explore topic models through word and topic correlations. We propose interactions to support user understanding, validation, and refinement of the models.

2 Group-in-a-box Layout for Visualizing a Relationship-Enriched Topic Model

Existing topic model visualizations do not easily support displaying the relationships between words in the topics and topics in the model. Instead, this requires a layout that supports intuitive visualization of nested network graphs. A group-in-a-box (GIB) layout (Rodrigues et al., 2011) is a network graph visualization that is ideal for our scenario as it is typically used for representing clusters with emphasis on the edges within and between clusters. The GIB layout visualizes subgraphs within a graph using a Treemap (Shneiderman, 1998) space filling technique and layout algorithms for optimizing the layout of sub-graphs within the space, such that related sub-graphs are placed together spatially. Figure 1 shows a sample group-in-a-box visualization.

We use the GIB layout to visually separate topics of the model as groups. We implement each topic as a force-directed network graph (Fruchterman and Reingold, 1991) where the nodes of the graph are the top words of the topic. An edge exists between two words in the network graph if the value of the term co-occurrence for the word pair is above a certain threshold,[2] and the edge is weighted by this value. Similarly, the edges between the topic clusters represent the topic covariance metric. Finally, the GIB layout optimizes the visualization such that related topic clusters are placed together spatially. The result is a topic visualization where related words are clustered within the topics and related topics are clustered within the overall layout.

[2]There are a variety of techniques for setting this threshold; currently, we aim to display fewer, stronger relationships to balance informativeness and complexity of the visualization

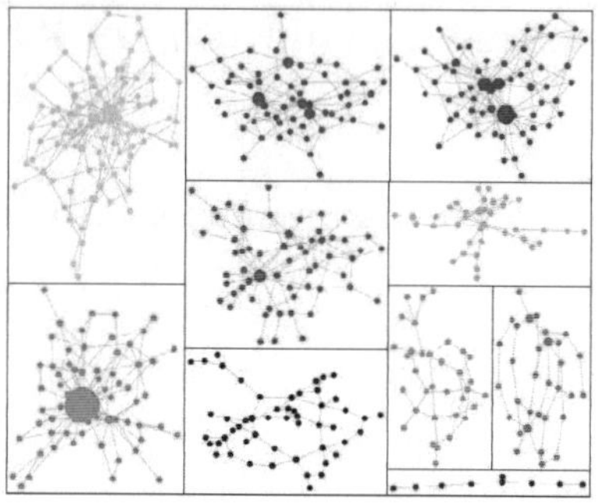

Figure 1: A sample GIB layout from (Rodrigues et al., 2011). The layout visualizes clusters distributed in a treemap structure where the partitions are based on the size of the clusters.

3 Relationship Metrics

We compute the term and topic relationship information required by the GIB layout as term co-occurrence and topic covariance, respectively. Term co-occurrence is a corpus-level statistic that can be computed independently from the LDA algorithm. The results of the LDA algorithm are required to compute the topic covariance.

3.1 Corpus-Level Term Co-Occurrence

Prior work has shown that Pointwise Mutual Information (PMI) is the most consistent scoring method for evaluating topic model coherence (Newman et al., 2010). PMI is a statistical technique for measuring the association between two observations. For our purposes, PMI is used to measure the correlation between each term pair within each topic on the document level[3]. The PMI is calculated for every possible term pair in the ingested data set using Equation 1. The visualization uses only the PMI for the term pairs for the top terms for each topic, which is a small subset of the calculated PMI values. Computing the PMI is trivial compared to the LDA calculation, and computing the values for all pairs allows the job to be run in parallel, as opposed to waiting for the results of the LDA job to determine the top term pairs.

$$PMI(x,y) = \log \frac{p(x,y)}{p(x)p(y)} \quad (1)$$

The PMI measure represents the probability of observing x given y and vice-versa. PMI can be

[3]We use document here, but the PMI can be computed at various levels of granularity as required by the analyst intent.

positive or negative, where 0 represents independence, and PMI is at its maximum when x and y are perfectly associated.

3.2 Topic Covariance

To quantify the relationship between topics in the model, we calculate the topic covariance metric for each pair of topics. To do this, we use the theta vector from the LDA output. The theta vector describes which topics are used for which documents in the model, where theta(d,i) represents how much the ith topic is expressed in document d. The equations for calculation the topic covariance are shown below.

$$\gamma_{di} = \frac{\theta_{di}}{\sum_j(\theta_{dj})} \tag{2}$$

$$\gamma_i = \frac{1}{D}\sum_d(\gamma_{di}) \tag{3}$$

$$\sigma(i,j) = \frac{1}{D}\sum_d(\gamma_{di} - \gamma_i)(\gamma_{dj} - \gamma_j)) \tag{4}$$

4 Visualization

The visualization represents the individual topics as network graphs where nodes represent terms and edges represent frequent term co-occurrence, and the layout of the topics represents topic covariance. The most *connected* topic is placed in the center of the layout, and the least connected topics are placed at the corners. Figure 2 shows the visualization for a topic model generated for a 1,000 document NSF dataset. As demonstrated in Figure 3, a user can hover over a topic to see the related topics[4]. In this example, the user has hovered over the {visualization, visual, interactive} topic, which is related to {user, interfaces}, {human, computer, interaction}, {design, tools}, and {digital, data, web} among others. Unlike other topical similarity measures, such as cosine similarity or a count of shared words, the topic covariance represents topics which are typically discussed together in the same documents, helping the user to discover semantically similar topics.

On the topic level, the size of the node in the topic network graph represents the probability of the word given the topic. By mapping word probability to the area of the nodes instead of the height

[4]we consider topics related if the topic co-occurrence is above a certain pre-defined threshold.

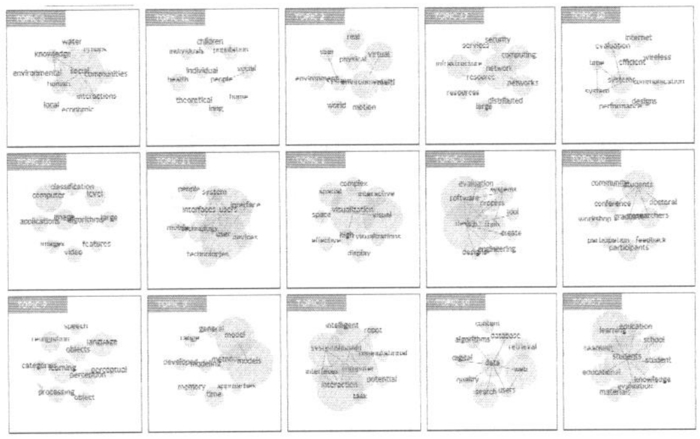

Figure 2: The visualization utilizes a group-in-a-box-inspired layout to represent the topic model as a nested network graph.

of words, the resulting visual encoding is not affected by the length of the words, a well-known issue with word cloud presentations that can visually bias longer terms. Furthermore, circles can overlap without affecting a user's ability to visually separate them, and lead to more compact and less cluttered visual layout. Hovering over a word node highlights the same word in other topics as shown in Figure 4.

This visualization is an alternative interface for Interactive Topic Modeling (ITM) (Hu et al., 2013). ITM presents users with topics that can be modified as appropriate. Our preliminary results show that topics containing highly-weighted sub-clusters may be candidates for splitting, whereas positively correlated topics are likely to be *good* topics, which do not need to be modified. In future work, we intend to perform an evaluation to show that this visualization enhances quality and efficiency of the ITM process.

To support user interactions required by the ITM algorithm, the visualization has an edit mode, which is shown in Figure 5. Ongoing work includes developing appropriate visual operations to support the following model-editing operations:

1. Adding words to a topic
2. Removing words from a topic
3. Requiring two words to be linked within a topic (must link)
4. Requiring two words to be forced into separate topics (cannot link)

5 Conclusion and Future Work

The visualization presented here provides a novel way to explore topic models with incorporated

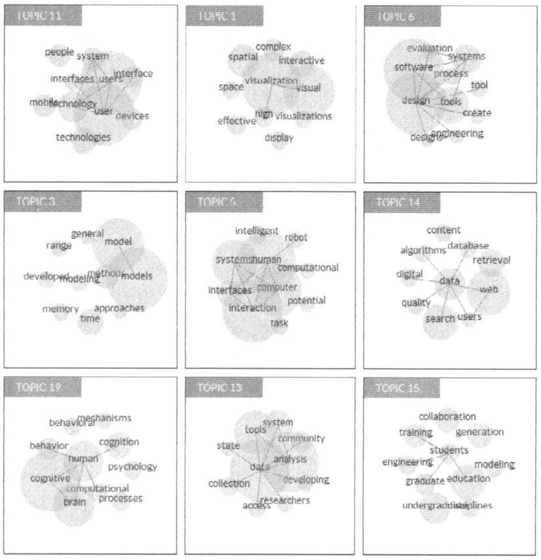

Figure 3: The user has hovered over the most-central topic in the layout, which is the most connected topic. The hovered topic is outlined, and the topic name is highlighted in turquoise. The topic names of the related topics are also highlighted.

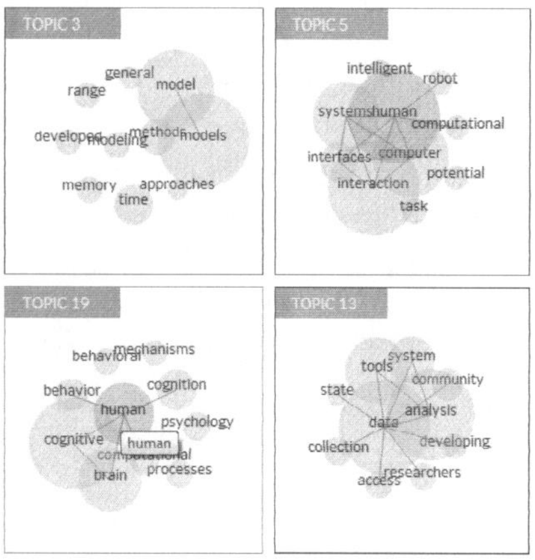

Figure 4: The visualization where the user has hovered over a word of interest. The same word is highlighted turquoise in other topics.

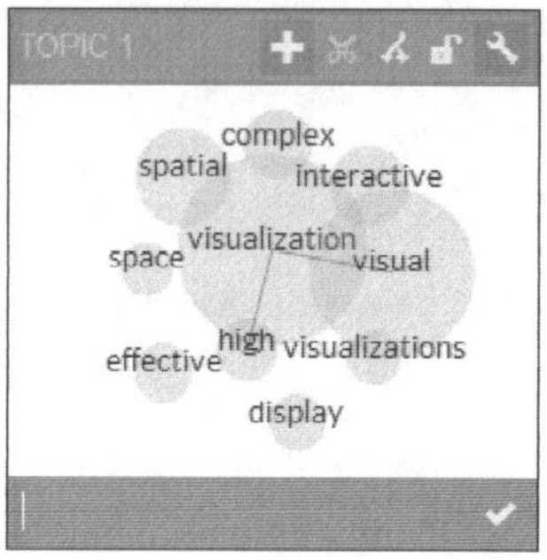

Figure 5: The edit mode for the visualization. From this mode, the user can add words, remove words, or rename the topic.

term and topic correlation information. This is a work in progress with the end goal to combine the visual representation with interactive topic modeling to allow users to explore (a) why a model may not align with their intuition and (b) modify the model as needed. We plan to deploy the tool on real-world domain users to iteratively refine the visualization and evaluate it in ecologically valid settings.

References

David M Blei, Andrew Y Ng, and Michael I Jordan. 2003. Latent dirichlet allocation. *Machine Learning Journal*, 3:993–1022.

Allison June-Barlow Chaney and David M Blei. 2012. Visualizing topic models. In *ICWSM*.

Jacob Eisenstein, Duen Horng Chau, Aniket Kittur, and Eric Xing. 2012. Topicviz: interactive topic exploration in document collections. In *CHI'12 Extended Abstracts*, pages 2177–2182. ACM.

Thomas MJ Fruchterman and Edward M Reingold. 1991. Graph drawing by force-directed placement. *Software: Practice and experience*, 21(11):1129–1164.

Matthew J Gardner, Joshua Lutes, Jeff Lund, Josh Hansen, Dan Walker, Eric Ringger, and Kevin Seppi. 2010. The topic browser: An interactive tool for browsing topic models. In *NIPS Workshop on Challenges of Data Visualization*.

Jacon Harris. 2011. Word clouds considered harmful. `http://www.niemanlab.org/2011/10/word-clouds-considered-harmful/`.

Yuening Hu, Jordan Boyd-Graber, Brianna Satinoff, and Alison Smith. 2013. Interactive topic modeling. *Machine Learning*, pages 1–47.

JD Lafferty and MD Blei. 2006. Correlated topic models. In *NIPS, Proceedings of the 2005 conference*, pages 147–155. Citeseer.

David Newman, Jey Han Lau, Karl Grieser, and Timothy Baldwin. 2010. Automatic evaluation of topic coherence. In *HLT*, pages 100–108. ACL.

Eduarda Mendes Rodrigues, Natasa Milic-Frayling, Marc Smith, Ben Shneiderman, and Derek Hansen. 2011. Group-in-a-box layout for multi-faceted analysis of communities. In *ICSM*, pages 354–361. IEEE.

Ben Shneiderman. 1998. Treemaps for space-constrained visualization of hierarchies.

Xuerui Wang, Andrew McCallum, and Xing Wei. 2007. Topical n-grams: Phrase and topic discovery, with an application to information retrieval. In *ICDM*, pages 697–702. IEEE.

Author Index